Elasticsearch Data Modeling and Schema Design

Rafid Reaz

Steve Hoberman

Align > Refine > Design Series

Technics Publications

Published by:

115 Linda Vista, Sedona, AZ 86336 USA
https://www.TechnicsPub.com

Edited by Sadie Hoberman
Cover design by Lorena Molinari
Illustrations by Joseph Shepherd
Contributions by Daniel Coupal and Pascal Desmarets

First Printing 2023
Copyright © 2023 by Technics Publications

ISBN, print ed.	9781634622950
ISBN, Kindle ed.	9781634622967
ISBN, ePub ed.	9781634622974
ISBN, PDF ed.	9781634622981

Library of Congress Control Number: 2023933989

Contents

List of Figures

List of Tables

About the Book

My daughter can make a mean brownie. She starts with a store-bought brownie mix and adds chocolate chips, apple cider vinegar, and other "secret" ingredients to make her own unique delicious brownie.

Building a robust database design meeting users' needs requires a similar approach. The store-bought brownie mix represents a proven recipe for success. Likewise, there are data modeling practices that have proven successful over many decades. The chocolate chips and other secret ingredients represent the special additions that lead to an exceptional product. Elasticsearch has a number of special design considerations, much like the chocolate chips. Combining proven data modeling practices with Elasticsearch design-specific practices creates a series of data models representing powerful communication tools, greatly improving the opportunities for an exceptional design and application.

In fact, each book in the Align > Refine > Design series covers conceptual, logical, and physical data modeling for a specific database product, combining the best of data modeling practices with solution-specific design considerations. It is a winning combination.

My daughter's first few brownies were not a success, although as the proud (and hungry) dad, I ate them anyway—and they were still pretty tasty. It took practice to get the brownie to come out amazing. We need practice on the modeling side as well. Therefore, each book in the series follows the same animal shelter case study, allowing you to see the modeling techniques applied to reinforce your learning.

If you want to learn how to build multiple database solutions, read all the books in the series. Once you read one, you can pick up the techniques for another database solution even quicker.

Some say my first word was "data." I have been a data modeler for over 30 years and have taught variations of my **Data Modeling Master Class** since 1992—currently up to the 10th Edition! I have written nine books on data modeling, including *The Rosedata Stone* and *Data Modeling Made Simple*. I review data models using my Data Model Scorecard® technique. I am the founder of the Design Challenges group, creator of the Data Modeling Institute's Data Modeling Certification exam, Conference Chair of the Data Modeling Zone conferences, director of Technics Publications, lecturer at Columbia University, and recipient of the Data Administration Management Association (DAMA) International Professional Achievement Award.

Thinking of my daughter's brownie analogy, I have perfected the store-bought brownie recipe. That is, I know how to model. However, I am not an expert in every database solution.

That is why each book in this series combines my proven data modeling practices with database solution experts. So, for this book, Rafid Reaz and I are making the brownie together. I work on the store-bought brownie piece, and Rafid works on adding the chocolate chips and other delicious ingredients. Rafid is an Elasticsearch thought leader.

Rafid entered the data modeling space at the young age of 22 after completing his undergraduate degree in Biology and Mathematics from the University of Ottawa. In July 2020, he became the 10th person worldwide and the first Canadian to enter the Data Modeling Institute's DMC Hall of Fame. He has experience creating and expanding standardized financial models and data delivery mechanisms using various modeling techniques. He also has experience in the data analytics and data science space, performing in-depth analysis and generating prediction models for Capital Markets, Retail Banking, and Insurance data. He has worked on both relational and NoSQL data models. Rafid spoke at the 2021 Data Modeling Zone Europe conference about reverse engineering physical NoSQL models to logical data models. In his spare time, Rafid enjoys recording music and creating digital art. Having a creative mind, he enjoys the process and innovation associated with data modeling.

We hope our tag team approach shows you how to model any Elasticsearch solution. Particularly for those with experience in data modeling of relational databases, the book provides a bridge from the traditional methods to the very different way we model to leverage the benefits of NoSQL in general and Elasticsearch in particular.

About Elasticsearch

Elasticsearch is an open search and analytics engine that supports multiple data types, including free-test, numerical, geospatial, structured, and unstructured. It has recently become a popular analytics solution due to ease-of-use, data distribution, speed, and scalability. Elasticsearch relies on the ability to index various types of data, which allows it to be used for many purposes, including application search, website search, enterprise search, logging, infrastructure metrics, performance monitoring, geospatial data analysis and visualization, security analytics, and business analytics to name a few.

In addition to the Elasticsearch engine, Elastic Stack is comprised of a few other tools:

- **Kibana**: Frontend application that sits on top of Elastic Stack, providing search and data visualization capabilities for data indexed in Elasticsearch.

- **Beats**: A platform used to send data from up to thousands of machines and systems to Logstash and Elasticsearch.

- **Logstash**: A server-side data processing pipeline that allows the collection of data from various sources, transforms them on the fly, and sends them to desired destinations. It serves as a data pipeline for Elasticsearch.

Companies of all sizes widely adopt Elastic Stack in various industries. Also, a large and active community of developers supports Elastic Stack. Elastic provides various support options and services to help customers use Elastic Stack.

The Elasticsearch Index

Let's look a bit more into how Elasticsearch works. Raw data flows into Elasticsearch from various sources, often using Logstash. Then comes the data ingestion phase, the process by which the raw data is parsed, normalized, and enriched before indexing. Once the data is indexed, users can run complex queries and use aggregation to retrieve summaries of the data. Then, using Kibana, users can create data visualizations, dashboards and manage the Elastic Stack.

One of the main components of Elasticsearch is the index. It is a collection of documents that are related to each other. Elasticsearch stores data as JSON documents. Each document is associated with a set of key/value pairs. It uses a data structure called an inverted index, which allows quick full-text searches by listing every unique word in a document and identifying all the documents that each word appears in. During indexing, Elasticsearch stores documents and builds an inverted index to make the data searchable and close to real-time.

Hence, its speed, distributed nature, wide set of features, simplified data ingestion, visualization, and reporting make Elastic Stack a widely sought-after analytics solution.

Two key features in a document-oriented database not found in tabular rows of Relational Database Management Systems (RDBMS) are hierarchical structures and polymorphism.[1] Let's review each.

Hierarchical structure in documents

Documents can represent data in a nested or hierarchical structure. This is in contrast with RDBMS tables, which are a two-dimensional tabular grid of columns and rows and require the use of relationships and joins to represent hierarchical data. In JSON documents, data can be nested within other data, creating a tree-like structure.

Aside from the traditional "scalar" data types (string, numeric, Boolean, null), it is possible to use what is known

---

[1] Relational databases have increasingly added support for JSON. But the capabilities are not the same as a pure document database, because in RDBMS, JSON payload is stored as a blob (or a varchar(4000)). As a result it lacks the indexing and query capabilities of Elasticsearch. PostgreSQL with its JSONB datatype is attempting to bridge that gap.

as "complex" data types: objects and arrays. In JSON, an object is a collection of key-value pairs enclosed in curly braces {}. See Figure 1.

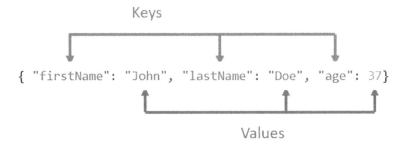

Figure 1: JSON object.

The keys are always strings, and the values can be any valid JSON data type, including another object, an array, a string, a number, a Boolean, or a null.

```
{
  "name": "John Smith",
  "age": 35,
  "address": {
    "street": "123 Main St",
    "city": "Anytown",
    "state": "CA",
    "zip": "12345"
  }
}
```

An array is an ordered list of values enclosed in square brackets []. The values can be any valid JSON data type, including another array, an object, a string, a number, a Boolean, or a null. Each value in the array is separated by a comma.

```
["apple",   "banana",   "orange",   "grape"]
```

You can combine objects and arrays at will, as shown in Figure 2.

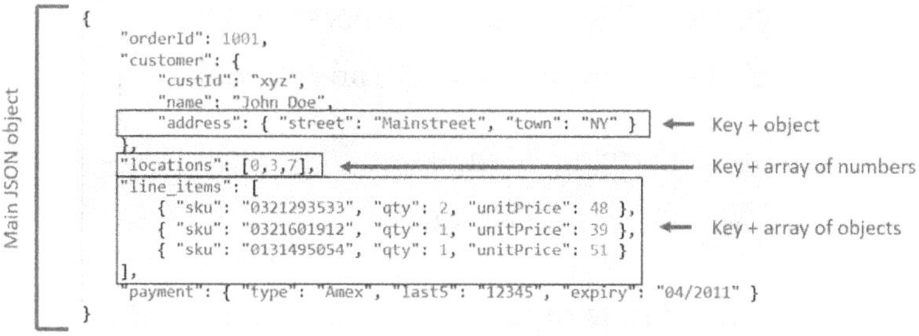

Figure 2: Combining objects at will.

For example, you may use an array of objects to embed another table into a collection. The array models the one-to-many or many-to-many relationship between the two tables.

Generally, the key is a static name in a JSON key-value pair. It is also possible to have variable names for the key:

```
{
    "followers": {
        "abc123": {
            "name": "John Doe",
            "sports": ["tennis"]
        },
        "xyz987": {
            "name": "Joe Blow",
            "sports": ["cycling", "football"]
        }
    }
}
```

This advanced feature, sometimes called "pattern properties" or "unpredictable keys, "is a special case of the attribute pattern detailed below. Hackolade Studio correctly maintains and detects these structures during the schema inference of a reverse-engineering process, but these unusual structures challenge traditional SQL and BI tools.

Grouping data in JSON with hierarchical subobjects and arrays can provide several benefits:

- **Improved data organization**: nesting related data with subobjects and arrays makes it easier to understand, navigate, query, and manipulate data.

- **Flexibility**: a more flexible data model can evolve and adapt to changing requirements more easily.

- **Improved performance**: embedding subdocuments within a parent document can improve performance by reducing the number of joins required to retrieve the data.

- **Better data representation**: for example, a customer object can contain a nested address object. In this way, it is clear that the address is related to the customer and is also more readable and intuitive.

- **Data integrity**: by keeping related data together, each order can contain an array of cart items. This way, it is clear that the orders and items are related, and it is also easy to update all related data when it is required and perform cascading deletes.

- **Developer convenience**: by aggregating structures to match objects to be manipulated in object-oriented programming, developers are more efficient by avoiding what's known as "object impedance mismatch," a common issue when working with relational databases.

Let's use the simple example of an order to fully visualize the above benefits and why users embrace the document model of Elasticsearch as an intuitive alternative to the traditional relational database structures.

With a relational database respecting normalization rules, we split the different components of an order into different tables at storage time. And when retrieving the data, joins are used to reassemble the different pieces for processing, display, or reporting. This is counter-intuitive for the common human (i.e., someone not trained in Third Normal Form) and expensive in terms of performance, particularly at scale. See Figure 3.

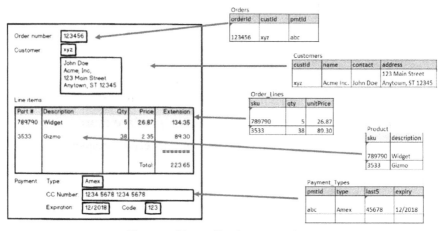

Figure 3: Normalization example.

However, with a JSON document, all the pieces of information that belong together are stored and retrieved in a single document, an example appearing in Figure 4. Nesting can provide the benefits described above, but it can also sometimes make data more complex and harder to work with if it's not properly organized and structured. And since there are no rules of normalization to serve as guardrails, data modeling is even more important than with relational databases.

Figure 4: JSON example.

Nesting subobjects and arrays to denormalize data to represent relationships can also increase the storage requirements. Still, with the minimal storage cost these days, this drawback is often considered marginal.

Just like XSD defines elements and structures that can appear in XML documents, JSON Schema (https://json-schema.org/) defines how a JSON document should be structured, making it easy to ensure it is formatted correctly. Elasticsearch is a schema-less engine. Hence, no data validation occurs before indexing the data. Sometimes, it's important to have the data validation done at the data store itself to ensure users get the correct data.

To decide whether to use or avoid, developers should weigh the benefits and drawbacks of nesting data and make an informed decision. Later in this book, the section about the different schema design patterns provides many details to help make informed decisions.

Polymorphism

Polymorphism in JSON refers to the ability of a JSON object to take on multiple forms.

Fields with multiple data types

The simplest case of polymorphism in JSON is when a field can have different data types, for example:

```
{
  "raceResults": [
      {
        "Position": 1,
        "Driver": "Lewis Hamilton"
      },
      {
        "Position": 2,
        "Driver": "Max Verstappen"
      },
      {
        "Position": "DNF",
        "Driver": "Charles Leclerc"
      }
  ]
}
```

The "Position" field can have different data types (numeric or string) depending on the race result.

Multiple document types in the same collection

A more complex case of polymorphism is when different documents in the same collection have different shapes, similar to table inheritance in relational databases. Specifically, it refers to the ability of a JSON object to have different properties or fields, depending on the type of data it represents.

For example, consider a collection for bank accounts. Several types of bank accounts are possible: checking, savings, and loan. There is a structure common to all types and a structure specific to each type. For example, a document for a checking account might look like this:

```
{
  "accountNumber": "123456789",
  "balance": 1000,
  "accountType": "checking",
  "accountDetails": {
    "minimumBalance": 100,
    "overdraftLimit": 500
  }
}
```

Another document for a savings account might look like this:

```
{
  "accountNumber": "987654321",
  "balance": 5000,
  "accountType": "savings",
  "accountDetails": {
    "interestRate": 0.05,
    "interestEarned": 115.26
  }
}
```

And for a loan account, a document might look like this:

```
{
  "accountNumber": "567890123",
  "balance": -5916.06,
  "accountType": "loan",
  "accountDetails": {
    "loanAmount": 10000,
    "term": 36,
    "interestRate": 1.5,
    "monthlyPmt": 291.71
  }
}
```

This flexible and dynamic structure is very convenient and eliminates the need for separate tables or wide tables that would quickly become unmanageable at scale.

However, this flexibility can also create challenges when querying or manipulating the data, as it requires applications to account for variations in data types and structure. Without going into details at this stage, Figure 5 shows a single schema for these documents.

Figure 5: Single schema.

For those familiar with traditional data modeling, the above would be represented with subtypes and could result in table inheritance, as shown in Figure 6.

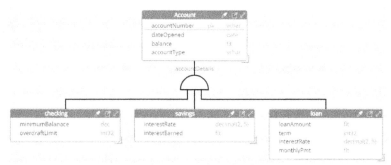

Figure 6: Subtyping.

Schema evolution and versioning

Another common case of polymorphism is when documents have different shapes within the same collection, due to the progressive evolution of the document schema over time. This could be done implicitly or with an explicit version number as part of the root-level fields of the document.

Developers love the fact that schema evolution is easy with Elasticsearch. You can add or remove fields, change data types, modify indexing options, etc., to accommodate new or changing requirements without the headaches that such changes would imply with relational databases. This gives developers the freedom and flexibility to make quick updates without going through a rigorous process.

The schema versioning pattern is described in detail later in this book. For now, it is enough to know that this pattern leverages the polymorphic capabilities of the document model.

We should manage schema evolution and versioning carefully to avoid technical debt and to consider that data may be read by different applications and SQL or BI tools that cannot handle this polymorphism. Schema migration is a best practice in successful projects and organizations leveraging NoSQL and, therefore, should be part of the schema evolution strategy to mitigate the drawbacks.

Elasticsearch Mapping

Another key concept within Elasticsearch is mapping. It is the process of defining how a document and the fields it contains are stored and indexed. Each document is made up of a set of fields, which each have their own data type. First, a mapping definition is created. This contains a list of fields in the document and metadata fields which control how the metadata associated with a document is handled. The process of defining a mapping helps optimize the performance of Elasticsearch and save disk space. Depending on how you define the type of each field, the field will be indexed and stored differently. There are two types of mapping within Elasticsearch: Dynamic and Explicit.

Dynamic Mapping

When a user does not define the mapping, Elasticsearch creates a default mapping known as dynamic mapping. Elasticsearch looks at each field and tries to infer the data type based on the content in that field. It then assigns a type to each field and creates a list of field names and types. This list is the mapping.

Explicit Mapping

Explicit mapping is when the user defines the mapping to create a list of fields and types associated with them.

Data modeling and schema design

As you can imagine, data modeling and schema design for Elasticsearch is very different than for relational databases. That's because Elasticsearch stores JSON-like documents as denormalized documents with nested objects and arrays instead of normalized flat tables. And also because Elasticsearch does not impose a fixed schema to be enforced by the database engine like a traditional RDBMS.

The flexibility of the document approach is a fantastic opportunity that many developers love. But this flexibility comes with some risks. As Elasticsearch does not enforce constraints, it is up to the developers to ensure that data remains consistent and conforms to application requirements. Failing to do so could lead to data corruption, inaccurate query results, and application errors. Data modeling helps mitigate these risks with a proactive approach to ensure that data is consistent and of high quality. It also contributes to higher productivity and lower Total Cost of Ownership (TCO). And with a modern approach to data modeling and next-gen tooling born in the 21st century, it fits right into your Agile development process.

Data modeling is a crucial step in the development process, as it allows developers to work closely with subject matter experts to define the structure of the data before any coding begins. Just as a recipe guides the baking of brownies, a data model serves as a blueprint for the structure and organization of data. By involving subject matter experts in the modeling process, developers can ensure that the data model accurately reflects the needs and requirements of the project. With such collaboration, developers are more likely to avoid potential mistakes and inconsistencies that could arise from working with poorly defined data. By following a recipe before starting to bake, developers can be more efficient and successful in creating a product that meets the needs of the end-user.

Audience

We wrote this book for two audiences:

- Data architects and modelers who need to expand their modeling skills to include Elasticsearch. That is, those of us who know how to make a store-bought brownie but are looking for those secret additions like chocolate chips.

- Database administrators and developers who know Elasticsearch but need to expand their modeling skills. That is, those of us who know the value of chocolate chips and other ingredients, but need to learn how to combine these ingredients with those store-bought brownie mixes.

This book contains a foundational introduction followed by three approach-driven chapters. Think of the introduction as making that store-built brownie and the subsequent chapters as adding chocolate chips and other yummy ingredients. More on these four sections:

- **Introduction: About Data Models**. This overview covers the three modeling characteristics of precise, minimal, and visual; the three model components of entities, relationships, and attributes; the three model levels of conceptual (align), logical (refine), and physical (design); and the three modeling perspectives of relational, dimensional, and query.

By the end of this introduction, you will know data modeling concepts and how to approach any data modeling assignment. This introduction will be useful to database administrators and developers who need a foundation in data modeling, as well as data architects and data modelers who need a modeling refresher.

- **Chapter 1: Align**. This chapter will explain the data modeling align phase. We explain the purpose of aligning our business vocabulary, introduce our animal shelter case study, and then walk through the align approach. This chapter will be useful for both audiences, architects/modelers, and database administrators/developers.

- **Chapter 2: Refine**. This chapter will explain the data modeling refine phase. We explain the purpose of refine, refine the model for our animal shelter case study, and then walk through the refine approach. This chapter will be useful for both audiences, architects/modelers and database administrators/developers.

- **Chapter 3: Design**. This chapter will explain the data modeling design phase. We explain the purpose of design, design the model for our animal shelter case study, and then walk through the design approach. This chapter will be useful for both audiences, architects/modelers and database administrators/developers.

We end each chapter with three tips and three takeaways. We aim to write as concisely yet comprehensively as possible to make the most of your time.

Most data models throughout the book were created using Hackolade Studio (https://hackolade.com) and are accessible for reference at https://github.com/hackolade/books, along with additional sample data models to play with.

Let's begin!

Rafid and Steve

About Data Models

This chapter is all about making that store-built brownie. We present the data modeling principles and concepts within a single chapter. In addition to explaining the data model, this chapter covers the three modeling characteristics of precise, minimal, and visual; the three model components of entities, relationships, and attributes; the three model levels of conceptual (align), logical (refine), and physical (design); and the three modeling perspectives of relational, dimensional, and query. By the end of this chapter, you will know how to approach any data modeling assignment.

Data model explanation

A model is a precise representation of a landscape. Precise means there is only one way to read a model—it is not ambiguous nor up to interpretation. You and I read the same model the exact same way, making the model an extremely valuable communication tool.

We need to 'speak' a language before we can discuss content. That is, once we know how to read the symbols on a model (syntax), we can discuss what the symbols represent (semantics).

Once we understand the syntax, we can discuss the semantics.

For example, a map like the one in Figure 7 helps a visitor navigate a city. Once we know what the symbols mean on a map, such as lines representing streets, we can read the map and use it as a valuable navigation tool for understanding a geographical landscape.

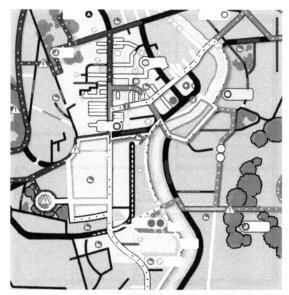

Figure 7: Map of a geographic landscape.

A blueprint like the one in Figure 8 helps an architect communicate building plans. The blueprint, too, contains only representations, such as rectangles for rooms and lines for pipes. Once we know what the rectangles and lines mean on a blueprint, we know what the structure will look like and can understand the architectural landscape.

The data model like the one in Figure 9 helps business and technologists discuss requirements and terminology. The data model, too, contains only representations, such as rectangles for terms and lines for business rules. Once we know what the rectangles and lines mean on a data model, we can debate and eventually agree on the business requirements and terminology captured in the informational landscape.

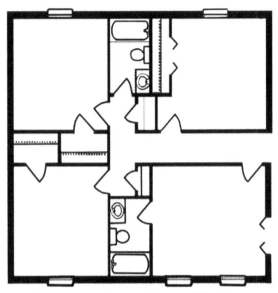

Figure 8: Map of an architectural landscape.

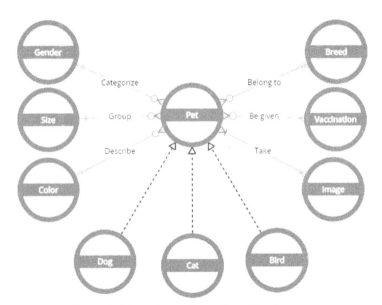

Figure 9: Map of an informational landscape.

A data model is a precise representation of an information landscape. We build data models to confirm and document our understanding of other perspectives.

In addition to precision, two other important characteristics of the model are minimal and visual. Let's discuss all three characteristics.

Three model characteristics

Models are valuable because they are precise—there is only one way to interpret the symbols on the model. We must transform the ambiguity in our verbal and sometimes written communication into a precise language. Precision does not mean complex—we need to keep our language simple and show the minimal amount needed for successful communication. In addition, following the maxim "a picture is worth a thousand words," we need visuals to communicate this precise and simple language for the initiative.

Precise, minimal, and visual are three essential characteristics of the model.

Precise

Bob: How's your course going?

Mary: Going well. But my students are complaining about too much homework. They tell me they have many other classes.

Bob: The attendees in my advanced session say the same thing.

Mary: I wouldn't expect that from graduates. Anyway, how many other offerings are you teaching this semester?

Bob: I'm teaching five offerings this term and one is an evening not-for-credit class.

We can let this conversation continue for a few pages, but do you see the ambiguity caused by this simple dialog?

- What is the difference between **Course**, **Class**, **Offering**, and **Session**?
- Are **Semester** and **Term** the same?
- Are **Student** and **Attendee** the same?

Precision means "exactly or sharply defined or stated." Precision means there is only one interpretation for a term, including the term's name, definition, and connections to other terms. Most issues organizations face related to growth, credibility, and saving lives, stem from a lack of precision.

On a recent project, Steve needed to explain data modeling to a group of senior human resource executives. These very high-level managers lead departments responsible for implementing a very expensive global employee expense system. Steve felt the last thing these busy human resource executives needed was a lecture on data modeling. So instead, he asked each of these managers sitting around this large boardroom table to write down their definition of an employee. After a few minutes, most of the writing stopped and he asked them to share their definitions of an employee.

As expected, no two definitions were the same. For example, one manager included contingency workers in his definition, while another included summer interns. Instead of spending the remaining meeting time attempting to come to a consensus on the meaning of an employee, we discussed the reasons we create data models, including the value of precision. Steve explained that after we complete the difficult journey of achieving the agreed-upon employee definition and document it in the form of a data model, no one will ever have to go through the same painful process again. Instead, they can use and build upon the existing model, adding even more value for the organization.

Making terms precise is hard work. We need to transform the ambiguity in our verbal and sometimes written communication into a form where five people can read about the term and each gets a single clear picture of the term, not five different interpretations. For example, a group of business users initially define **Product** as:

Something we produce intending to sell for profit.

Is this definition precise? If you and I read this definition, are we each clear on what *something* means? Is *something* tangible like a hammer or instead some type of service? If it is a hammer and we donate this hammer to a not-for-profit organization, is it still a hammer? After all, we didn't make a *profit* on it. The word *intending* may cover us, but still, shouldn't this word be explained in more detail? And who is *we*? Is it our entire organization or maybe just a subset? What does *profit* really mean anyway? Can two people read the word *profit* and see it very differently?

You see the problem. We need to think like a detective to find gaps and ambiguous statements in the text to make terms precise. After some debate, we update our **Product** definition to:

A product, also known as a finished product, is something that is in a state to be sold to a consumer. It has completed the manufacturing process, contains a wrapper, and is labeled for resale. A product is different than a raw material and a semi-finished good. A raw material such as sugar or milk, and a semi-finished good such as melted chocolate is never sold to a consumer. If in the future, sugar or milk is sold directly to consumers, than sugar and milk become products.

Examples:
Widgets Dark Chocolate 42 oz
Lemonizer 10 oz
Blueberry pickle juice 24 oz

Ask at least five people to see if they are all clear on this particular initiative's definition of a product. The best way to test precision is to try to break the definition. Think of lots of examples and see if everyone makes the same decision as to whether the examples are products or not.

In 1967, G.H. Mealy wrote a white paper where he made this statement:

> We do not, it seems, have a very clear and commonly agreed upon set of notions about data—either what they are, how they should be fed and cared for, or their relation to the design of programming languages and operating systems.[2]

---

[2] G. H. Mealy, "Another Look at Data," AFIPS, pp. 525-534, 1967 Proceedings of the Fall Joint Computer Conference, 1967.

Although Mr. Mealy made this claim over 50 years ago, if we replace *programming languages and operating systems* with the word *databases*, we can make a similar claim today.

Aiming for precision can help us better understand our business terms and business requirements.

Minimal

The world around us is full of obstacles that can overwhelm our senses, making it very challenging to focus only on the relevant information needed to make intelligent decisions. Therefore, the model contains a minimal set of symbols and text, simplifying a subset of the real world by only including representations of what we need to understand.

Much is filtered out on a model, creating an incomplete but extremely useful reflection of reality. For example, we might need to communicate descriptive information about **Customer**, such as their name, birth date, and email address. But we will not include information on the process of adding or deleting a customer.

---

http://tw.rpi.edu/media/2013/11/11/134fa/GHMealy-1967-FJCC-p525.pdf.

Visuals

Visuals mean that we need a picture instead of lots of text. Our brains process images 60,000 times faster than text, and 90 percent of the information transmitted to the brain is visual.[3]

We might read an entire document but not reach that moment of clarity until we see a figure or picture summarizing everything. Imagine reading directions to navigate from one city to another versus the ease of reading a map that shows visually how the roads connect.

Three model components

The three components of a data model are entities, relationships, and attributes (including keys).

Entities

An entity is a collection of information about something important to the business. It is a noun considered basic and critical to your audience for a particular initiative. Basic means this entity is mentioned frequently in conversations

---

[3] https://www.t-sciences.com/news/humans-process-visual-data-better.

while discussing the initiative. Critical means the initiative would be very different or non-existent without this entity.

The majority of entities are easy to identify and include nouns that are common across industries, such as **Customer**, **Employee**, and **Product**. Entities can have different names and meanings within departments, organizations, or industries based on audience and initiative (scope). An airline may call a **Customer** a *Passenger*, a hospital may call a **Customer** a *Patient*, an insurance company may call a **Customer** a *Policyholder*, yet they are all recipients of goods or services.

Each entity fits into one of six categories: who, what, when, where, why, or how. That is, each entity is either a who, what, when, where, why, or how. Table 1 contains a definition of each of these categories, along with examples.

Entities are traditionally shown as rectangles on a data model, such as these two for our animal shelter:

Figure 10: Traditional entities.

Entity instances are the occurrences, examples, or representatives of that entity. The entity **Pet** may have multiple instances, such as Spot, Daisy, and Misty. The entity **Breed** may have multiple instances, such as German Shephard, Greyhound, and Beagle.

Category	Definition	Examples
Who	Person or organization of interest to the initiative.	Employee, Patient, Player, Suspect, Customer, Vendor, Student, Passenger, Competitor, Author
What	Product or service of interest to the initiative. What the organization makes or provides that keeps it in business.	Product, Service, Raw Material, Finished Good, Course, Song, Photograph, Tax Preparation, Policy, Breed
When	Calendar or time interval of interest to the initiative.	Schedule, Semester, Fiscal Period, Duration
Where	Location of interest to the initiative. Location can refer to actual places as well as electronic places.	Employee Home Address, Distribution Point, Customer Website
Why	Event or transaction of interest to the initiative.	Order, Return, Complaint, Withdrawal, Payment, Trade, Claim
How	Documentation of the event of interest to the initiative. Records events such as a Purchase Order (a "How") recording an Order event (a "Why"). A document provides evidence that an event took place.	Invoice, Contract, Agreement, Purchase Order, Speeding Ticket, Packing Slip, Trade Confirmation

Table 1: Entity categories plus examples.

Entities and entity instances take on more precise names when discussing specific technologies. For example, entities are tables and instances are rows in a RDBMS like Oracle.

Entities are collections and instances are documents in Elasticsearch.

Relationships

A relationship represents a business connection between two entities, and appears on the model traditionally as a line connecting two rectangles. For example, here is a relationship between **Pet** and **Breed**:

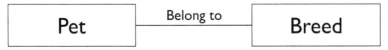

Figure 11: Relationship and label.

The phrase **Belong to** is called a *label*. A label adds meaning to the relationship. Instead of just saying that a **Pet** may relate to a **Breed**, we can say that a **Pet** may belong to a **Breed**. **Belong to** is more meaningful than **Relate**.

So far, we know that a relationship represents a business connection between two entities. It would be nice to know more about the relationship, such as whether a **Pet** may belong to more than one **Breed** or whether a **Breed** can categorize more than one **Pet**. Enter cardinality.

Cardinality means the additional symbols on the relationship line that communicate how many instances from one entity participate in the relationship with instances of the other entity.

There are several modeling notations, and each notation has its own set of symbols. Throughout this book, we use a notation called *Information Engineering (IE)*. The IE notation has been a very popular notation since the early 1980s. If you use a notation other than IE within your organization, you must translate the following symbols into the corresponding symbols in your modeling notation.

We can choose any combination of zero, one, or many for cardinality. *Many* (some people use "more") means one or more. Yes, many includes one. Specifying one or many allows us to capture *how many* of a particular entity instance participate in a given relationship. Specifying zero or one allows us to capture whether an entity instance is or is not required in a relationship.

Recall this relationship between **Pet** and **Breed**:

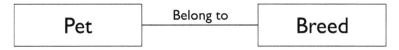

Figure 12: Relationship and label.

Let's now add cardinality.

We first ask the *Participation* questions to learn more. Participation questions tell us whether the relationship is 'one' or 'many.' So, for example:

- Can a **Pet** belong to more than one **Breed**?
- Can a **Breed** categorize more than one **Pet**?

A simple spreadsheet can keep track of these questions and their answers:

Question	Yes	No
Can a Pet belong to more than one Breed?		
Can a Breed categorize more than one Pet?		

We asked the animal shelter experts and received these answers:

Question	Yes	No
Can a Pet belong to more than one Breed?	✓	
Can a Breed categorize more than one Pet?	✓	

We learn that a **Pet** may belong to more than one **Breed**. For example, Daisy is part Beagle and part Terrier. We also learned that a **Breed** may categorize more than one **Pet**. Both Sparky and Spot are Greyhounds. 'Many' (meaning one or more) on a data model in the IE notation is a symbol that looks like a crow's foot (and is called a *crow's foot* by data folks). See Figure 13.

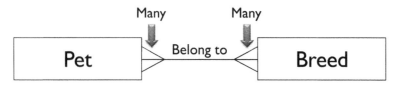

Figure 13: Displaying the answers to the Participation questions.

Now we know more about the relationship:

- Each **Pet** may belong to many **Breeds**.
- Each **Breed** may categorize many **Pets**.

We also always use the word 'each' when reading a relationship and start with the entity that makes the most sense to the reader, usually the one with the clearest relationship label.

This relationship is not yet precise, though. So, in addition to asking these two Participation questions, we also need to ask the *Existence* questions. Existence tells us for each relationship whether one entity can exist without the other term. For example:

- Can a **Pet** exist without a **Breed**?
- Can a **Breed** exist without a **Pet**?

We asked the animal shelter experts and received these answers:

Question	Yes	No
Can a Pet exist without a Breed?		✓
Can a Breed exist without a Pet?	✓	

So we learn that a **Pet** cannot exist without a **Breed**, and that a **Breed** can exist without a **Pet**. This means, for example, that we may not have any Chihuahuas in our animal shelter. Yet we need to capture a **Breed** (and in this case, one or more **Breeds**), for every **Pet**. As soon as we know about Daisy, we need to identify at least one of her breeds, such as Beagle or Terrier.

Figure 14 displays the answers to these two questions.

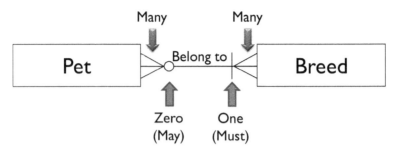

Figure 14: Displaying the answers to the Existence questions.

After adding existence, we have a precise relationship:

- Each **Pet** must belong to many **Breeds**.
- Each **Breed** may categorize many **Pets**.

The Existence questions are also known as the May/Must questions. The Existence questions tell us when reading the relationship, whether we say "may" or "must." A zero means "may," indicating optionality—the entity can exist without the other entity. A **Breed** *may* exist without a **Pet**, for example. A one means "must," indicating required—the entity cannot exist without the other entity. A **Pet** *must* belong to at least one **Breed**, for example.

Two more questions need to be asked if we are working on the more detailed logical data model (which will be discussed shortly). These are the *Identification* questions. Identification tells us for each relationship whether one entity can be identified without the other term. For example:

- Can a **Pet** be identified without a **Breed**?
- Can a **Breed** be identified without a **Pet**?

We asked the animal shelter experts and received these answers:

Question	Yes	No
Can a Pet be identified without a Breed?	✓	
Can a Breed be identified without a Pet?	✓	

So we learn that a **Pet** can be identified without knowing a **Breed**. We can identify the pet Sparky without knowing that Sparky is a German Shepherd. In addition, we can identify a **Breed** without knowing the **Pet**. This means, for example, that we can identify the Chihuahua breed without including any information from **Pet**.

A dotted line captures a non-identifying relationship. That is, when the answer to both questions is "yes." A solid line captures an identifying relationship. That is, when one of the answers is "no."

Non-identifying

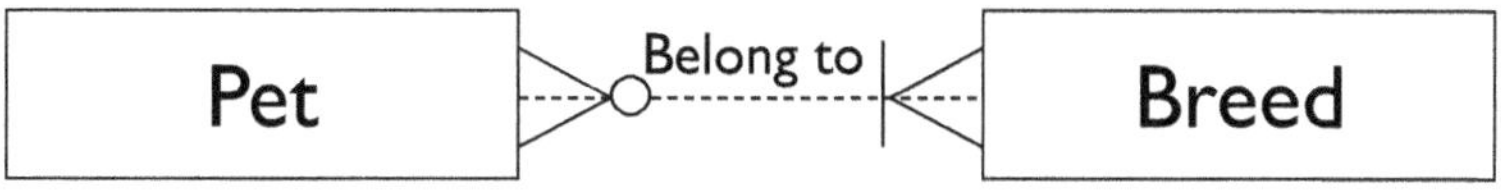

Identifying

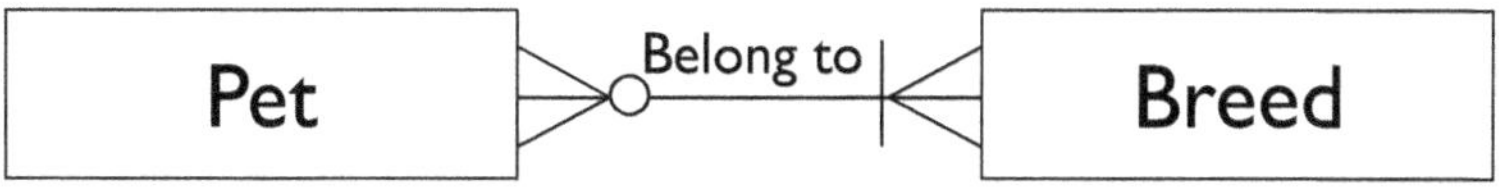

Figure 15: A non-identifying (top) and identifying (bottom) relationship.

So to summarize, the Participation questions reveal whether each entity has a one or many relationship to the other entity. The Existence questions reveal whether each entity has an optional ("may") or mandatory ("must") relationship to the other entity. The Identification questions reveal whether each entity requires the other entity to bring back a unique entity instance.

Use instances to make things clear in the beginning and eventually help you explain your models to colleagues. See Figure 16 for an example.

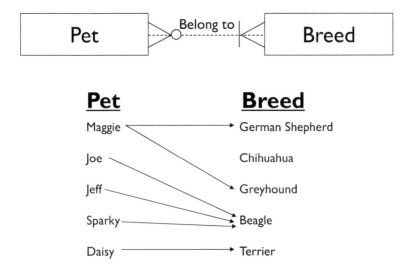

Figure 16: Use sample data to validate a relationship.

You can see from this dataset that a **Pet** can belong to more than one **Breed**, such as Maggie being a German Shepherd/Greyhound mix. You can also see that every **Pet** must belong to at least one **Breed**. We could also have a

Breed that is not categorizing any **Pets**, such as Chihuahua. In addition, a **Breed** can categorize multiple **Pets**, such as Joe, Jeff, and Sparky are all Beagles.

Answering all six questions leads to a precise relationship. Precise means we all read the model the same exact way.

Let's say that we have slightly different answers to our six questions:

Question	Yes	No
Can a Pet belong to more than one Breed?		✓
Can a Breed categorize more than one Pet?	✓	
Can a Pet exist without a Breed?		✓
Can a Breed exist without a Pet?	✓	
Can a Pet be identified without a Breed?	✓	
Can a Breed be identified without a Pet?	✓	

These six answers lead to this model:

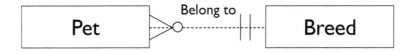

- Each **Pet** must belong to one **Breed**.
- Each **Breed** may categorize many **Pets**.

Figure 17: Different answers to the six questions lead to different cardinality.

In this model, we are only including pure-breed pets, as a **Pet** must be assigned one **Breed**. No mutts in our shelter!

Be very clear on labels. Labels are the verbs that connect our entities (nouns). To read any complete sentence, we need both nouns and verbs. Make sure the labels on the relationship lines are as descriptive as possible. Here are some examples of good labels:

- Contain
- Provide
- Own
- Initiate
- Characterize

Avoid the following words as labels, as they provide no additional information to the reader. You can use these words in combination with other words to make a meaningful label; just avoid using these words by themselves:

- Have
- Associate
- Participate
- Relate
- Are

For example, replace the relationship sentence:

"Each **Pet** must *relate to* one **Breed**."

With:

"Each **Pet** must *belong to* one **Breed**."

Relationships take on more precise names when discussing specific technologies. For example, relationships are constraints in a RDBMS such as Oracle. Relationships in Elasticsearch can be represented with references, but they are not enforceable constraints. It is often preferred to implement relationships through embedding. The pros and cons of both approaches are discussed at length later in the book. In addition to relationship lines, we can also have a subtyping relationship. The subtyping relationship groups common entities together. For example, the **Dog** and **Cat** entities might be grouped using subtyping under the more generic **Pet** term. In this example, **Pet** would be called the grouping entity or supertype, and **Dog** and **Cat** would be the terms that are grouped together, also known as the subtypes, as shown in Figure 18.

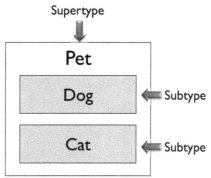

Figure 18: Subtyping is similar to the concept of inheritance.

We would read this model as:

- Each **Pet** may be either a **Dog** or a **Cat**.
- **Dog** is a **Pet**. **Cat** is a **Pet**.

The subtyping relationship means that all of the relationships (and attributes that we'll learn about shortly) that belong to the supertype from other terms also belong to each subtype. Therefore, the relationships to **Pet** also belong to **Dog** and **Cat**. So, for example, cats can be assigned breeds as well, so the relationship to **Breed** can exist at the **Pet** level instead of the **Dog** level, encompassing both cats and dogs. See Figure 19 for an example.

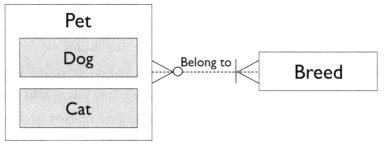

Figure 19: The relationship to Pet is inherited to Dog and Cat.

So the relationship:

- Each **Pet** must belong to many **Breeds**.
- Each **Breed** may categorize many **Pets**.

Also applies to **Dog** and **Cat**:

- Each **Dog** must belong to many **Breeds**.
- Each **Breed** may categorize many **Dogs**.
- Each **Cat** must belong to many **Breeds**.
- Each **Breed** may categorize many **Cats**.

Not only does subtyping reduce redundancy, but it also makes it easier to communicate similarities across what would appear to be distinct and separate terms.

Attributes and keys

An entity contains attributes. An *attribute* is an individual piece of information whose values identify, describe, or measure instances of an entity. The entity **Pet** might contain the attributes **Pet Number** that identifies the **Pet**, **Pet Name** that describes the **Pet**, and **Pet Age** that measures the **Pet**.

Attributes take on more precise names when discussing specific technologies. For example, attributes are columns in a RDBMS such as Oracle. Attributes are fields in Elasticsearch.

A candidate key is one or more attributes that uniquely identify an entity instance. We assign a **ISBN** (International Standard Book Number) to every title. The **ISBN** uniquely identifies each title and is, therefore, the title's candidate key. **Tax ID** can be a candidate key for an organization in some countries, such as the United States. **Account Code** can be a candidate key for an account. A **VIN** (Vehicle Identification Number) identifies a vehicle.

A candidate key must be unique and mandatory. Unique means a candidate key value must not identify more than one entity instance (or one real-world thing). Mandatory means a candidate key cannot be empty (also known as *nullable*). Each entity instance must be identified by exactly one candidate key value.

The number of distinct values of a candidate key is always equal to the number of distinct entity instances. If the entity **Title** has **ISBN** as its candidate key, and if there are 500 title instances, there will also be 500 unique ISBNs.

Even though an entity may contain more than one candidate key, we can only select one candidate key to be the primary key for an entity. A primary key is a candidate key chosen to be *the preferred* unique identifier for an entity. An alternate key is a candidate key that, although it has the properties of being unique and mandatory, was not chosen as the primary key though it may still be used to find specific entity instances.

The primary key appears above the line in the entity box, and the alternate key contains the 'AK' in parentheses. So in the following **Pet** entity, **Pet Number** is the primary key and **Pet Name** is the alternate key. Having an alternate key on **Pet Name** means we cannot have two pets with the same name. Whether this can happen or not is a good discussion point. However, the model in its current state would not allow duplicate **Pet Names**.

Figure 20: An alternate key on Pet Name means we cannot have two pets with the same name.

A candidate key can be either simple, compound, or composite. If it is simple, it can be either business or surrogate. Table 2 contains examples of each key type.

	SIMPLE	COMPOUND	COMPOSITE	OVERLOADED
BUSINESS	ISBN	PROMOTION TYPE CODE PROMOTION START DATE	(CUSTOMER FIRST NAME + CUSTOMER LAST NAME + BIRTHDAY)	STUDENT GRADE
SURROGATE	BOOK ID			

Table 2: Examples of each key type.

Sometimes a single attribute identifies an entity instance, such as **ISBN** for a title. When a single attribute makes up a key, we use the term *simple key*. A simple key can be a business (also called natural) key or a surrogate key.

A business key is visible to the business (such as **Policy Number** for a **Policy**). A surrogate key is never visible to the business. A surrogate key is created by a technologist to help with a technology issue, such as space efficiency, speed, or integration. It is a unique identifier for a table, often a counter, usually fixed-size, and always system-generated without intelligence, so a surrogate key carries no business meaning.

Sometimes it takes more than one attribute to uniquely identify an entity instance. For example, both a **Promotion Type Code** and **Promotion Start Date** may be necessary to identify a promotion. When more than one attribute makes up a key, we use the term *compound key*. Therefore, **Promotion Type Code** and **Promotion Start Date** together are a compound candidate key for a promotion. When a key contains more than one piece of information, we use the term *composite key*. A simple key that includes the customer's first name, last name, and birthday, all in the same attribute, would be an example of a simple composite key. When a key contains different attributes, it is called an *overloaded* key. A **Student Grade** attribute might sometimes contain the actual grade, such as A, B, or C. At other times it might just contain a P for Pass and F for Fail. **Student Grade**, therefore, would be an overloaded attribute. **Student Grade** sometimes contains the student's grade, and other times indicates whether the student has passed the class.

Let's look at the model in Figure 21.

Figure 21: The entity on the many side contains a foreign key pointing back to the primary key from the entity on the one side.

Here are the rules captured on this model:

- Each **Gender** may categorize many **Pets**.
- Each **Pet** must be categorized by one **Gender**.
- Each **Pet** may Receive many **Vaccinations**.
- Each **Vaccination** may be given to many **Pets**.

The entity on the "one" side of the relationship is called the parent entity, and the entity on the "many" side of the relationship is called the child entity. For example, in the relationship between **Gender** and **Pet**, **Gender** is the parent and **Pet** is the child. When we create a relationship from a parent entity to a child entity, the parent's primary key is copied as a foreign key to the child. You can see the foreign key, **Gender Code**, in the **Pet** entity.

A foreign key is one or more attributes that link to another entity (or, in a case of a recursive relationship where two instances of the same entity may be related, that is, a relationship that starts and ends with the same entity, a link to the same entity). At the physical level, a foreign key allows a relational database management system to navigate from one table to another. For example, if we need to know the **Gender** of a particular **Pet**, we can use the **Gender Code** foreign key in **Pet** to navigate to the parent **Gender**.

Three model levels

Traditionally, data modeling produces a set of structures for a Relational Database Management System (RDBMS). First, we build the Conceptual Data Model (CDM) (more appropriately called the Business Terms Model or BTM for short) to capture the common business language for the initiative (e.g., "What's a Customer?"). Next, we create the Logical Data Model (LDM) using the BTM's common business language to precisely define the business requirements (e.g., "I need to see the customer's name and address on this report."). Finally, in the Physical Data Model (PDM), we design these business requirements specific for a particular technology such as Oracle, Teradata, or SQL Server (e.g., "Customer Last Name is a variable length not null field with a non-unique index..."). Our PDM represents the RDBMS design for an application. We then generate the Data Definition Language (DDL) from the PDM, which we can run within a RDBMS environment to create the set of tables that will store the application's data. To summarize, we go from common business language to business requirements to design to tables.

Although the conceptual, logical, and physical data models have played a very important role in application development over the last 50 years, they will play an even more important role over the next 50 years.

Regardless of the technology, data complexity, or breadth of requirements, there will always be a need for a diagram that captures the business language (conceptual), the business requirements (logical), and the design (physical).

The names *conceptual*, *logical*, and *physical*, however, are deeply rooted in the RDBMS side. Therefore, we need more encompassing names to accommodate both RDBMS and NoSQL for all three levels.

Align = Conceptual, Refine = Logical, Design = Physical

Using the terms Align, Refine, and Design instead of Conceptual, Logical, and Physical has two benefits: greater purpose and broader context.

Greater purpose means that by rebranding into Align, Refine, and Design, we include what the level does in the name. Align is about agreeing on the common business vocabulary so everyone is *aligned* on terminology and general initiative scope. Refine is about capturing the business requirements. That is, refining our knowledge of the initiative to focus on what is important. Design is about the technical requirements. That is, making sure we accommodate the unique needs of software and hardware on our model.

Broader context means there is more than just the models. When we use terms such as conceptual, most project teams only see the model as the deliverable, and do not recognize all of the work that went into producing the model or other related deliverables such as definitions, issue/question resolutions, and lineage (lineage meaning where the data comes from). The align phase includes the conceptual (business terms) model, the refine phase includes the logical model, and the design phase includes the physical model. We don't lose our modeling terms. Instead, we distinguish the model from its broader phase. For example, instead of saying we are in the logical data modeling phase, we say we are in the refine phase, where the logical data model is one of the deliverables. The logical data model exists within the context of the broader refine phase.

However, if you are working with a group of stakeholders who may not warm up to the traditional names of conceptual, logical, and physical, you can call the conceptual the *alignment model*, the logical the *refinement model*, and the physical the *design model*. Use the terms that would have the largest positive impact on your audience.

The conceptual level is Align, the logical Refine, and the physical Design. Align, Refine, and Design—easy to remember and even rhymes!

Business terms (Align)

We have had many experiences where people who need to speak a common business language do not consistently use the same set of terms. For example, Steve recently facilitated a discussion between a senior business analyst and a senior manager at a large insurance company.

The senior manager expressed his frustration on how a business analyst was slowing down the development of his business analytics application. "The team was meeting with the product owner and business users to complete the user stories on insurance quotes for our upcoming analytics application on quotes, when a business analyst asked the question, *What is a quote?* The rest of the meeting was wasted on trying to answer this question. Why couldn't we just focus on getting the Quote Analytics requirements, which we were in that meeting to do? We are supposed to be Agile!"

If there was a lengthy discussion trying to clarify the meaning of a quote, there is a good chance this insurance company does not understand a quote well. All business users may agree that a quote is an estimate for a policy premium but disagree at what point an estimate becomes a quote. For example, does an estimate have to be based on a certain percentage of facts before it can be considered a quote?

How well will Quote Analytics meet the user requirements if the users are not clear as to what a *quote* is? Imagine needing to know the answer to this question:

How many life insurance quotes were written last quarter in the northeast?

Without a common alignment and understanding of *quote*, one user can answer this question based on their definition of *quote*, and someone else can answer based on their different definition of *quote*. One of these users (or possibly both) will most likely get the wrong answer.

Steve worked with a university whose employees could not agree on what a *student* meant, a manufacturing company whose sales and accounting departments differed on the meaning of *return on total assets*, and a financial company whose analysts battled relentlessly over the meaning of a *trade*—it's all the same challenge we need to overcome, isn't it?

It's about working towards a common business language.

A common business language is a prerequisite for success in any initiative. We can capture and communicate the terms underlying business processes and requirements, enabling people with different backgrounds and roles to understand and communicate with each other.

A Conceptual Data Model (CDM), more appropriately called a Business Terms Model (BTM), is a language of symbols and text that simplifies an informational landscape by providing a precise, minimal, and visual tool scoped for a particular initiative and tailored for a particular audience.

This definition includes the need to be well-scoped, precise, minimal, and visual. Knowing the type of visual that will have the greatest effectiveness requires knowing the audience for the model.

The audience includes the people who will validate and use the model. Validate means telling us whether the model is correct or needs adjustments. Use means reading and benefiting from the model. The scope encompasses an initiative, such as an application development project or a business intelligence program.

Knowing the audience and scope helps us decide which terms to model, what the terms mean, how the terms relate to each other, and the most beneficial type of visual.

Additionally, knowing the scope ensures we don't "boil the ocean" and model every possible term in the enterprise. Instead, only focusing on those that will add value to our current initiative.

Although this model is traditionally called a *conceptual data model*, the term "conceptual" is often not received as a very positive term by those outside the data field. "Conceptual" sounds like a term the IT team would come up with. Therefore, we prefer to call the "conceptual data model" the "business terms model" and will use this term going forward. It is about business terms, and including the term "business" raises its importance as a business-focused deliverable and also aligns with data governance.

A business terms model often fits nicely on a single piece of paper—and not a plotter-size paper! Limiting a BTM to one page is important because it encourages us to select only key terms. We can fit 20 terms on one page but not 500 terms.

Being well-scoped, precise, minimal, and visual, the BTM provides a common business language. As a result, we can capture and communicate complex and encompassing business processes and requirements, enabling people with different backgrounds and roles to initially discuss and debate terms, and to eventually communicate effectively using these terms.

With more and more data being created and used, combined with intense competition, strict regulations, and rapid-spread social media, the financial, liability, and credibility stakes have never been higher. Therefore the need for a common business language has never been greater. For example, Figure 22 contains a BTM for our animal shelter.

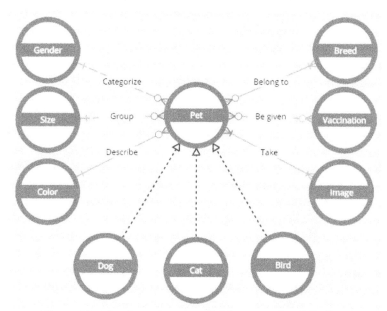

Figure 22: A business terms model for our animal shelter.

Each of these entities will have a precise and clear definition. For example, **Pet** might have a similar definition to what appears in Wikipedia:

A pet, or companion animal, is an animal kept primarily for a person's company or entertainment rather than as a working animal, livestock, or a laboratory animal.

More than likely, though, there will be something about the definition that provides more meaning to the reader of a particular data model and is more specific to a particular initiative, such as:

A pet is a dog, cat, or bird that has passed all the exams required to secure adoption. For example, if Sparky has passed all of his physical and behavioral exams, we would consider Sparky a pet. However, if Sparky has failed at least one exam, we will label Sparky an animal that we will reevaluate later.

Let's now walk through the relationships:

- Each Pet may be either a Dog, Cat, or Bird.
- Dog is a Pet.
- Cat is a Pet.
- Bird is a Pet.
- Each Gender may categorize many Pets.
- Each Pet must be categorized by one Gender.
- Each Size may group many Pets.
- Each Pet must be grouped by one Size.
- Each Color may describe many Pets.
- Each Pet must be described by one Color.
- Each Pet must belong to many Breeds.
- Each Breed may categorize many Pets.
- Each Pet may be given many Vaccinations.
- Each Vaccination may be given to many Pets.
- Each Pet must take many Images.
- Each Image must be taken of many Pets.

Logical (Refine)

A logical data model (LDM) is a business solution to a business problem. It is how the modeler refines the business requirements without complicating the model with implementation concerns such as software and hardware.

For example, after capturing the common business language for a new order application on a BTM, the LDM will refine this model with attributes and more detailed relationships and entities to capture the requirements for this order application. The BTM would contain definitions for **Order** and **Customer**, and the LDM would contain the **Order** and **Customer** attributes needed to deliver the requirements.

Returning to our animal shelter example, Figure 23 contains a subset of the logical data model for our animal shelter.

Figure 23: Logical data model subset for our animal shelter.

The requirements for our shelter application appear on this model. This model shows the attributes and relationships needed to deliver a solution to the business. For example, in the **Pet** entity, each **Pet** is identified by a **Pet Number** and described by its name and gender. **Gender** and **Vaccination** are defined lists. We also capture that a **Pet** must have one **Gender** and can receive any number (including zero) of **Vaccinations**.

Note that an LDM in the context of relational databases respects the rules of normalization. Hence in the above diagram, there are associative entities, also known as "junction tables," which prepare for the physical implementation of many-to-many relationships.

Since Elasticsearch allows us to embed and denormalize, we often don't need these "junction tables" and opt for a simpler view of the same business rules. We can keep together what belongs together, following the Domain-Driven Design concept of "aggregates" discussed below, and leveraging denormalization. See Figure 24.

Figure 24: This denormalized representation can easily lead to a normalized physical data model, whereas the opposite is not necessarily true in more complex configurations.

An important part of the requirements-gathering exercise is identifying, quantifying, and qualifying the workload by recording frequency of queries, latency of results, volume and velocity of data, retentions, etc. This is discussed in more detail in the Refine chapter.

Domain-Driven Design

It is useful at this stage to briefly cover a popular methodology used in software development: Domain-Driven Design. Its principles have some relevance in the context of data modeling for NoSQL.

Eric Evans is the author of the book, *Domain-Driven Design: Tackling Complexity in the Heart of Software*, published in 2003, which is considered one of the most influential works on Domain-Driven Design (DDD). Its principles include:

- **Ubiquitous language**: establishing a common language used by all stakeholders of a project, and reflecting the concepts and terms that are relevant to the business.

- **Bounded context**: managing the complexity of the system by breaking it down into smaller, more manageable pieces. This is done by defining a boundary around each specific domain of the software system. Each bounded context has its own model and language that is appropriate for that context.

- **Domain model**: using a business terms model of the domain that represents the important entities, their relationships, and the behaviors of the domain.

- **Context mapping**: defining and managing the interactions and relationships between different bounded contexts. Context mapping helps to ensure that different models are consistent with each other and that communication between teams is effective.

- **Aggregates**: identifying clusters of related objects, and treating each of them as a single unit of change. Aggregates help to enforce consistency and integrity within a domain.

- **Continuous refinement**: an iterative process with continuous refinement of the domain model as new insights and requirements are discovered. The domain model should evolve and improve over time based on feedback from stakeholders and users.

These principles are striking by their common sense and are applicable to enhance data modeling. Yet, the nuances are important. For example, we have seen that a BTM helps build a common vocabulary. DDD pushes further for developers to use this language in the code and in the name of collections/tables and fields/columns.

Some data modeling traditionalists have expressed reservations about DDD (and also about Agile development.) For every methodology and technology, there are, of course, examples of misinterpretation and misguided efforts. But applied with clairvoyance and experience, DDD and Agile can lead to great success. We see DDD principles as directly applicable to data modeling to further enhance its relevance, rather than as an opposite approach.

In the context of NoSQL databases and modern architecture patterns and stacks, including event-driven and micro-services, DDD is particularly relevant. Specifically, the DDD concept of "aggregates" matches the hierarchical nature of JSON documents with nested objects and denormalization. As a result, the strict definition of a logical data model is too constraining as it implies that the technology-agnostic model respects the rules of normalization. Hackolade has extended the capabilities of its technology-agnostic models to allow complex data types for nesting and denormalization in Polyglot data models to accommodate the support of NoSQL structures.

Physical (Design)

The physical data model (PDM) is the logical data model compromised for specific software or hardware. The BTM captures our common business vocabulary, the LDM our business requirements, and the PDM our technical requirements. That is, the PDM is a data model of our business requirements structured to work well with our technology. The physical represents the technical design.

While building the PDM, we address the issues that have to do with specific hardware or software, such as, how can we best design our structures to:

- Process this operational data as quickly as possible?
- Make this information secure?
- Answer these business questions with a sub-second response?

Figure 25 contains a relational version and Figure 26 a nested version of a subset of the PDM for our animal shelter:

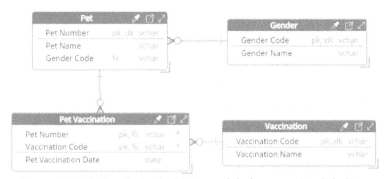

Figure 25: Relational physical data models for our animal shelter.

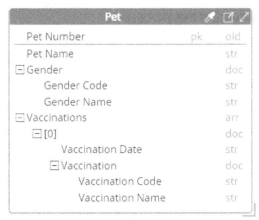

Figure 26: Nested physical data models for our animal shelter.

We have compromised our logical model to work with specific technology. For example, if we are implementing in a RDBMS such as Oracle, we might need to combine (denormalize) structures together to make retrieval performance acceptable.

Figure 25 is a normalized RDBMS model and Figure 26 shows one possible denormalization to leverage the document approach of Elasticsearch. Information belonging together is kept together with the nesting of subobjects. The cardinality of the relational junction table Pet Vaccination is replaced by an array to store multiple Vaccinations. This aggregation approach enables the referential integrity of the atomic unit of each document. Note that the nesting does not prevent the existence of a Vaccination table if an access pattern in the application requires it, but would then require synchronization of the denormalized data to ensure consistency.

Three model perspectives

Relational Database Management System (RDBMS) and NoSQL are the two main modeling perspectives. Within the RDBMS, the two settings are relational and dimensional. Within NoSQL, the one setting is query. Therefore, the three modeling perspectives are relational, dimensional, and query. Table 3 contrasts relational, dimensional, and query. This section goes into more detail into each perspective.

Factor	Relational	Dimensional	Query
Benefit	Precisely representing data through sets	Precisely representing how data will be analyzed	Precisely representing how data will be received and accessed
Focus	Business rules *constraining* a business process	Business questions *analyzing* a business process	Access paths *providing insights* into a business process
Use case	Operational (OLTP)	Analytics (OLAP)	Discovery
Parent perspective	RDBMS	RDBMS	NoSQL
Example	A Customer must own at least one Account.	How much revenue did we generate in fees by Date, Region, and Product? Also want to see by Month and Year…	Which customers own a checking account that generated over $10,000 in fees this year, own at least one cat, and live within 500 miles of New York City?

Table 3: Comparing relational, dimensional, and query.

A RDBMS stores data in sets based on Ted Codd's groundbreaking white papers written from 1969 through 1974. Codd's ideas were implemented in the RDBMS with tables (entities at the physical level) containing attributes. Each table has a primary key and foreign key constraints to enforce the relationships between tables. The RDBMS has been around for so many years primarily because of its ability to retain data integrity by enforcing rules that maintain high-quality data. Secondly, the RDBMS enables efficiency in storing data, reducing redundancy, and saving storage space at the cost of using more CPU power. Over the last decade, the benefit of saving space has diminished as disks get cheaper while CPU performance is not improving. Both trajectories favor NoSQL databases these days.

NoSQL means "NoRDBMS." A NoSQL database stores data differently than a RDBMS. A RDBMS stores data in tables (sets) where primary and foreign keys drive data integrity and navigation. A NoSQL database does not store data in sets. For example, Elasticsearch stores data in JSON format. Other NoSQL solutions may store data in Resource Description Framework (RDF) triplesExtensible Markup Language (XML), or Binary Encoded JavaScript Object Notation (BSON).

Relational, dimensional, and query can exist at all three model levels, giving us nine different types of models, as shown in Table 4. We discussed the three levels of Align,

Refine, and Design in the previous section. We align on a common business language, refine our business requirements, and then design our database. For example, if we are modeling a new claims application for an insurance company, we might create a relational model capturing the business rules within the claims process. The BTM would capture the claims business vocabulary, the LDM would capture the claims business requirements, and the PDM would capture the claims database design.

	RELATIONAL	DIMENSIONAL	NoSQL
BUSINESS TERMS (ALIGN)	TERMS AND RULES	TERMS AND PATHS	TERMS AND QUERIES
LOGICAL (REFINE)	SETS	MEASURES WITH CONTEXT	QUERY-FOCUSED HIERACHY
PHYSICAL (DESIGN)	COMPROMISED SETS	STAR SCHEMA OR SNOWFLAKE	ENHANCED HIERACHY

Table 4: Nine different types of models.

Relational

Relational models work best when there is a requirement to capture and enforce business rules. For example, a relational model may be ideal if an operational application requires applying many business rules, such as an order application ensuring that every order line belongs to one and only one order, and that each order line is identified by its order number plus a sequence number. The relational perspective focuses on business rules.

We can build a relational at all three levels: business terms, logical, and physical. The relational business terms model contains the common business language for a particular initiative. Relationships capture the business rules between these terms. The relational logical data model includes entities along with their definitions, relationships, and attributes. The relational physical data model includes physical structures such as tables, columns, and constraints. The business terms, logical, and physical data models shared earlier are examples of relational. See Figure 27, Figure 28, and Figure 29.

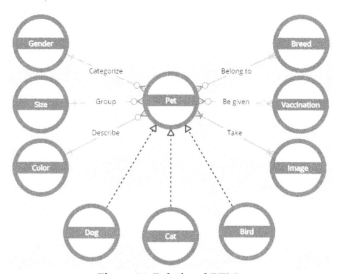

Figure 27: Relational BTM.

Figure 28: Relational LDM.

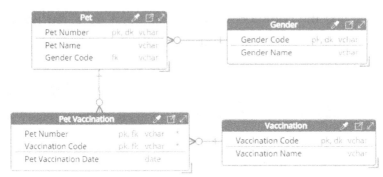

Figure 29: Relational PDM.

Figure 30 contains another example of a BTM.

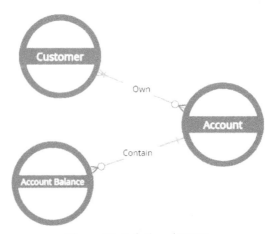

Figure 30: Relational BTM.

The relationships capture that:

- Each **Customer** may own many **Accounts.**
- Each **Account** must be owned by many **Customers.**
- Each **Account** may contain many **Account Balances.**
- Each **Account Balance** must belong to one **Account.**

We wrote the following definitions during one of our meetings with the project sponsor:

Customer	A customer is a person or organization who has opened one or more accounts with our bank. If members of a household each have their own account, each member of a household is considered a distinct customer. If someone has opened an account and then closed it, they are still considered a customer.
Account	An account is a contractual arrangement by which our bank holds funds on behalf of a customer.
Account Balance	An account balance is a financial record of how much money a customer has in a particular account with our bank at the end of a given time period, such as someone's checking account balance at the end of a month.

For the relational logical data model, we assign attributes to entities (sets) using a set of rules called *normalization*.

Although normalization has a foundation in mathematics (set theory and predicate calculus), we see it more as a technique to design a flexible structure. More specifically, we define normalization as a process of asking business questions, increasing your knowledge of the business and enabling you to build flexible structures that support high-quality data.

The business questions are organized around levels, including First Normal Form (1NF), Second Normal Form (2NF), and Third Normal Form (3NF). These three levels have been neatly summarized by William Kent:

Every attribute depends upon the key, the whole key, and nothing but the key, so help me Codd.

"Every attribute depends upon the key" is 1NF, "the whole key" is 2NF, and "nothing but the key" is 3NF. Note that the higher levels of normalization include the lower levels, so 2NF includes 1NF, and 3NF includes 2NF and 1NF.

To make sure that every attribute depends upon the key (1NF), we need to make sure for a given primary key value, we get at most one value back from each attribute. For example, **Author Name** assigned to a **Book** entity would violate 1NF because for a given book, such as this book, we can have more than author. Therefore **Author Name** does not belong to the **Book** set (entity) and needs to be moved to a different entity. More than likely, **Author Name** will be assigned to the **Author** entity, and a relationship will exist between **Book** and **Author,** stating among other things, that a **Book** can be written by more than one **Author.**

To make sure every attribute depends upon the whole key (2NF), we need to make sure we have the minimal primary key. For example, if the primary key for **Book** was both **ISBN** and a **Book Title**, we would quickly learn that **Book Title** is not necessary to have in the primary key. An attribute such as **Book Price** would depend directly on the **ISBN,** and therefore including **Book Title** in the primary key would not add any value.

To make sure there are no hidden dependencies ("nothing but the key," which is 3NF), we need to make sure every attribute depends directly on the primary key and nothing else. For example, the attribute **Order Gross Amount** does not depend directly on the primary key of **Order** (most likely, **Order Number**). Instead, **Order Gross Amount** depends upon **List Price** and **Item Quantity,** which are used to derive the **Order Gross Amount**.

Data Modeling Made Simple, by Steve Hoberman, goes more into detail into each of the levels of normalization, including the levels above 3NF. Realize the main purpose of normalization is to correctly organize attributes into sets. Also, note that the normalized model is built according to the properties of the data and not built according to how the data is being used.

Dimensional models are built to answer specific business questions with ease, and NoSQL models are built to answer queries and identify patterns with ease. The relational model is the only model focused on the intrinsic properties of the data and not usage.

Dimensional

A dimensional data model captures the business *questions* behind one or more business processes. The answers to the questions are metrics, such as **Gross Sales Amount** and **Customer Count**.

A dimensional model is a data model whose only purpose is to allow efficient and user-friendly filtering, sorting, and summing of measures. That is, analytics applications. The relationships on a dimensional model represent navigation paths instead of business rules, as with the relational model. The scope of a dimensional model is a collection of related measures plus context that together address some business process. We build dimensional models based upon one or more business questions that evaluate a business process. We parse the business questions into measures and ways of looking at these measures to create the model.

For example, suppose we work for a bank and would like to better understand the fee generation process. In that case, we might ask the business question, "What is the total amount of fees received by **Account Type** (such as Checking or Savings), **Month**, **Customer Category** (such as Individual or Corporate), and **Branch**?" See Figure 31. This model also communicates the requirement to see fees not just at a **Month** level but also at a **Year** level, not just a **Branch** level, but also at a **Region** and **District** level.

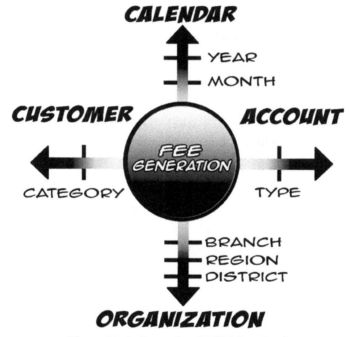

Figure 31: A dimensional BTM for a bank.

Term definitions:

Fee Generation	Fee generation is the business process where money is charged to customers for the privilege to conduct transactions against their account, or money charged based on time intervals, such as monthly charges to keep a checking account open that has a low balance.
Branch	A branch is a physical location open for business. Customers visit branches to conduct transactions.
Region	A region is our bank's own definition of dividing a country into smaller pieces for branch assignment or reporting purposes.
District	A district is a grouping of regions used for organizational assignments or reporting purposes. Districts can and often do cross country boundaries, such as North America and Europe districts.
Customer Category	A customer category is a grouping of one or more customers for reporting or organizational purposes. Examples of customer categories are Individual, Corporate, and Joint.
Account Type	An account type is a grouping of one or more accounts for reporting or organizational purposes. Examples of account types are Checking, Savings, and Brokerage.
Year	A year is a period of time containing 365 days, consistent with the Gregorian calendar.
Month	A month is each of the twelve named periods into which a year is divided.

You might encounter terms such as **Year** and **Month** which are commonly understood terms, and therefore minimal time can be invested in writing a definition. Make sure, though, that these are commonly understood terms, as sometimes even **Year** can have multiple meanings, such as whether the reference is to a fiscal or standard calendar.

Fee Generation is an example of a meter. A meter represents the business process that we need to measure. The meter is so important to the dimensional model that the name of the meter is often the name of the application: the **Sales** meter, the Sales Analytics Application. **District, Region**, and **Branch** represent the levels of detail we can navigate within the **Organization** dimension. A *dimension* is a subject whose purpose is to add meaning to the measures. For example, **Year** and **Month** represent the levels of detail we can navigate within the **Calendar** dimension. So this model contains four dimensions: **Organization, Calendar, Customer**, and **Account**.

Suppose an organization builds an analytical application to answer questions on how a business process is performing, such as a sales analytics application. Business questions become very important in this case, so we build a dimensional data model. The dimensional perspective focuses on business questions. We can build a dimensional data model at all three levels: business terms, logical, and physical. Figure 31 displayed our business terms model, Figure 32 shows the logical, and Figure 33 the physical.

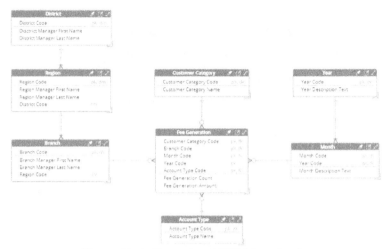

Figure 32: A dimensional LDM for a bank.

Figure 33: A dimensional PDM for a bank.

Query

Suppose an organization builds an application to discover something new about a business process, such as a fraud detection application. Queries become very important in that case, so we build a query data model.

We can build a query data model at all three levels: business terms, logical, and physical. Figure 34 contains a query business terms model, Figure 35 and Figure 36 the query logical data models, and Figure 37 the query physical data model.

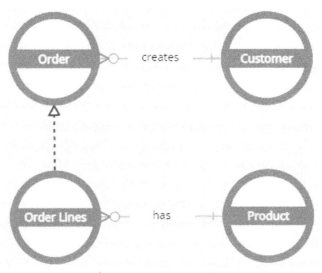

Figure 34: A query BTM.

The Query BTM does not look any different from other BTMs as the vocabulary and scope are the same, independent of the physical database implementation. In fact, we can even ask the Participation and Existence questions for each relationship in our query BTM, if we feel that it would add value. In the above example:

- a **Customer** creates an **Order**
- an **Order** is made of **Order Lines**
- an **Order Line** has a **Product**

It is possible to toggle the display of attributes for the different entities.

When it comes to the logical model, however, access patterns and workload analysis dictate the model. Depending on whether there are queries for maintenance screens for Customers and Products, you could have the strictly embedded logical model in Figure 35, or the model in Figure 36.

The first logical model would lead to a single collection in Elasticsearch, whereas it will be automatically normalized into three tables when instantiated to a physical model for a relational database.

Figure 35: Strictly embedded logical model.

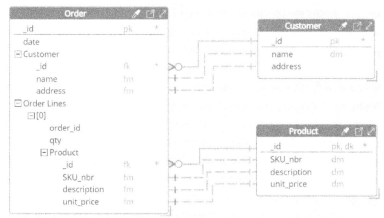

Figure 36: A query LDM.

The second logical model will lead to three collections in Elasticsearch to accommodate the maintenance of **Customers** and **Products**, but keeping the **Order** table as an aggregate combines embedding and referencing schema design patterns.

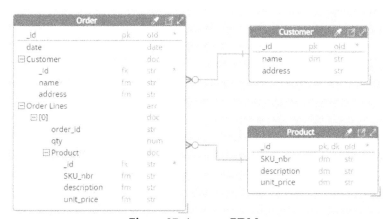

Figure 37: A query PDM.

In the above model, we show nesting, denormalization, and referencing. Nesting allows aggregating information that belongs together in a user-friendly structure to make it easily understandable by humans. Denormalization is implemented so a query to retrieve an order would fetch all of the necessary information in a single seek, without having to execute expensive joins, even if it is a repetition of the data in the master collections Customer and Product. Access patterns might still be required to view and update Customer and Product information regardless of the orders to which they might be linked. Therefore, we keep the master Customer collection and the master Product collection. In the Order collection, we keep a reference to the master document. Since there is no cross-document referential integrity built into the database engine, the responsibility to maintain the synchronization shifts to the application or to an offline process, such as a Logstash pipeline.

One final remark: there could be a good reason not to update a denormalized piece of information. For example, the ship-to address of an already fulfilled order should not be updated because a customer moves to a new address. Only pending orders should be updated. Denormalization is sometimes more precise than cascading updates.

CHAPTER 1

Align

This chapter will explain the data modeling align phase. We explain the purpose of aligning our business vocabulary, introduce our animal shelter case study, and then walk through the align approach. We end this chapter with three tips and three takeaways.

Purpose

The align stage aims to capture a common business vocabulary within a business terms model for a particular initiative.

For NoSQL models, you might use a different term than a business terms model, such as a *query alignment model*. We also like this term, which is more specific to the purpose of a NoSQL BTM, as our goal is modeling the queries.

Our animal shelter

A small animal shelter needs our help. They currently advertise their ready-to-adopt pets on their own website. They use a Microsoft Access relational database to keep track of their animals, and they publish this data weekly on their website. See Figure 38 for their current process.

A Microsoft Access record is created for each animal after the animal passes a series of intake tests and is deemed ready for adoption. The animal is called a pet once it is ready for adoption.

Once a week, the pet records are updated on the shelter's website. New pets are added and adopted pets have been removed.

Figure 38: Animal shelter current architecture.

Not many people know about this shelter, and, therefore, animals often remain unadopted for much longer than the national average. Consequently, they would like to partner with a group of animal shelters to form a consortium where all of the shelters' pet information will appear on a much more popular website. Our shelter will need to extract data from their current MS Access database and migrate it into Elasticsearch. Data can be migrated from MS Access to an Elasticsearch index using a built-in ODBC driver called UCanAccess and a data processing pipeline Logstash which ingests data into Elasticsearch from many sources. Elasticsearch would be the back-end using Search UI, which is a web-based search engine with pre-built connectors for Elasticsearch, as the front end.

Let's now look at the shelter's current models. The animal shelter built the business terms model (BTM) in Figure 39 to capture the common business language for the initiative.

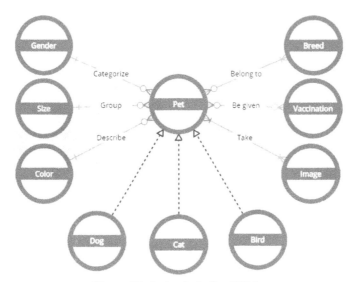

Figure 39: Animal shelter BTM.

In addition to this diagram, the BTM also contains precise definitions for each term, such as this definition **Pet** mentioned earlier in the chapter:

A pet is a dog, cat, or bird that has passed all the exams required to secure adoption. For example, if Sparky has passed all of his physical and behavioral exams, we would consider Sparky a pet. However, if Sparky has failed at least one exam, we will label Sparky an animal that we will reevaluate later.

Our animal shelter knows its world well and has built fairly solid models. Recall that a subset of the data will be migrated into Elasticsearch using built-in ODBC drivers and can later be displayed and queried using Search UI. Let's go through the align, refine, and design approach for the Elasticsearch Index.

Approach

The align stage is about developing the initiative's common business vocabulary. We will follow the steps shown in Figure 40.

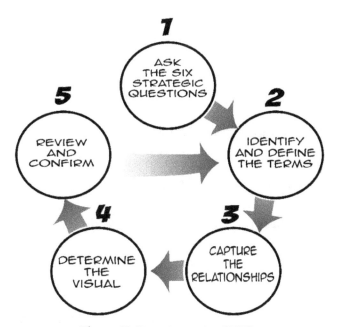

Figure 40: Steps to create a BTM.

Before you begin any project, we must ask six strategic questions (Step 1). These questions are a prerequisite to the success of any initiative because they ensure we choose the right terms for our BTM. Next, identify all terms within the scope of the initiative (Step 2). Make sure each term is clearly and completely defined. Then determine how these terms are related to each other (Step 3). Often, you will need to go back to Step 2 at this point because in capturing relationships, you may come up with new terms. Next, determine the most beneficial visual for your audience (Step 4). Consider the visual that would resonate best with those that will need to review and use your BTM. As a final step, seek approval of your BTM (Step 5). Often at this point, there are additional changes to the model, and we cycle through these steps until the model is accepted.

Let's build a BTM following these five steps.

Step 1: Ask the six strategic questions

Six questions must be asked to ensure a valuable BTM. These questions appear in Figure 41.

1. **What is our initiative?** This question ensures we know enough about the initiative to determine the scope. Knowing the scope allows us to decide which terms should appear on the initiative's BTM. Eric Evans, in his book *Domain-Driven Design*,

introduces the concept of "Bounded Context," which is all about understanding and defining your scope. For example, terms such as **Animal, Shelter Employee**, and **Pet Food** are out of scope.

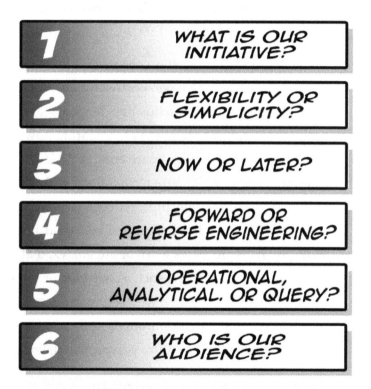

Figure 41: Six questions to ensure model success.

2. **Flexibility or simplicity?** This question ensures we introduce generic terms only if there is a need for flexibility. Generic terms allow us to accommodate new types of terms that we do not know about today and also allow us to better group similar terms together. For example, **Person** is flexible and

Employee is simple. **Person** can include other terms we have not yet considered, such as **Adopter, Veterinarian**, and **Volunteer**. However, **Person** can be a more difficult term to relate to than **Employee.** We often describe our processes using business-specific terms like **Employee.**

3. **Now or later?** This question ensures we have chosen the correct time perspective for our BTM. BTMs capture a common business language at a point in time. If we are intent on capturing how business processes work or are analyzed today, then we need to make sure terms, along with their definitions and relationships, reflect a current perspective (now). If we are intent on capturing how business processes work or are analyzed at some point in the future, such as one year or three years into the future, then we need to make sure terms, along with their definitions and relationships, reflect a future perspective (later).

4. **Forward or reverse engineering?** This question ensures we select the most appropriate "language" for the BTM. If business requirements drive the initiative, then it is a forward engineering effort and we choose a business language. It does not matter whether the organization is using SAP or Siebel, the BTM will contain business terms. If an application is driving the initiative, then it is a

reverse engineering effort and we choose an application language. If the application uses the term **Object** for the term **Product**, it will appear as **Object** on the model and be defined according to how the application defines the term, not how the business defines the term. As another example of reverse engineering, you might have as your starting point some type of physical data structure, such as a database layout, an XML, or a JSON document. For example, the following JSON snippet might reveal the importance of **Shelter Volunteer** as a business term:

```
{
  "name": "John Smith",
  "age": 35,
  "address": {
    "street": "123 Main St",
    "city": "Anytown",
    "state": "CA",
    "zip": "12345"
  }
}
```

5. **Operational, analytics, or query?** This question ensures we choose the right type of BTM— relational, dimensional, or query. Each initiative requires its respective BTM.

6. **Who is our audience?** We need to know who will review our model (validator) and who will use our model going forward (users).

1. *What is our initiative?*

Mary is the animal shelter volunteer responsible for intake. Intake is the process of receiving an animal and preparing the animal for adoption. She has been a volunteer for over ten years, and was the main business resource in building the original Microsoft Access database.

She is enthusiastic about the new initiative, seeing it as a way to get animals adopted in less time. We might start off by interviewing Mary, where the goal is to have a clear understanding of the initiative, including its scope:

> **You**: Thanks for making time to meet with me. This is just our first meeting, and I don't want to keep you behind our allocated time, so let's get right to the purpose of our interview and then a few questions. The earlier we identify our scope and then define the terms within this scope, the greater the chance for success. Can you please share with me more about this initiative?
>
> **Mary**: Sure! The main driver for our initiative is to make our furry friends get adopted faster. Today on average, our pets are adopted in two weeks. We and other small local shelters would like to get this down to five days on average. Maybe even less, hope so. We will send our pet data to a consortium we have formed with other local shelters to centralize our listings and reach a wider audience.
>
> **You**: Do you have all types of pets, or just dogs and cats?

Mary: I'm not sure what kinds of pets the other shelters have other than dogs and cats, but we also have birds up for adoption.

You: Ok, and are there any pets to exclude from this initiative?

Mary: Well, it takes a few days for an animal to be assessed to be considered ready for adoption. We run some tests and sometimes procedures. I like to use the term pet when an animal has completed these processes and is now ready for adoption. So we do have animals that are not yet pets. We are only including pets in this initiative.

You: Got it. And when somebody is looking for a furry best friend, what kinds of filters would they use?

Mary: I've talked with volunteers at the other shelters too. We feel after filtering first on the type of pet, such as dog, cat, or bird, filtering by breed, gender, color, and size would be the most important filters.

You: What kinds of information would someone expect to see when clicking on a pet description that was returned by the filter selections?

Mary: Lots of images, a cute name, maybe information on the pet's color or breed. That sort of thing.

You: Makes sense. What about people? Do you care about people as part of this initiative?

Mary: What do you mean?

You: Well, the people who drop off pets and the people who adopt pets.

Mary: Yes, yes. We keep track of this information. By the way, the people who drop off animals we call surrenderers, and the people who adopt pets are adopters. We are not sending any person details to the consortium. We don't see it relevant and don't want to risk getting sued over privacy issues. Spot the dog will never sue us, but Bob the surrenderer might.

You: I can understand that. Well, I think I understand the scope of the initiative, thank you.

We now have a good understanding of the scope of the initiative. It includes all pets (not all animals) and no people. As we refine the terminology, we might have more questions for Mary around scope.

2. Flexibility or simplicity?

Let's continue the interview to answer the next question.

You: Flexibility or simplicity?

Mary: I don't understand the question.

You: We need to determine whether to use generic terms or, for lack of a better word, more concrete terms. Using generic terms, such as mammal instead of **dog** or **cat,** allows us to accommodate future terms later, such as other kinds of mammals like monkeys or whales.

Mary: We haven't had many whales up for adoption this month. [laughs]

You: Ha!

Mary: Flexibility sounds appealing, but we shouldn't go overboard. I can see eventually we might have other kinds of pets, so a certain level of flexibility would be useful here. But not too much. I remember working on the Microsoft Access system and someone was trying to get us to use a Party concept to capture dogs and cats. It was too hard for us to get our heads around it. Too fuzzy, if you know what I mean.

You: I do know what you mean. Ok, a little flexibility to accommodate different kinds of pets, but not to go overboard. Got it.

3. Now or later?

Now on to the next question.

> **You**: Should our model reflect how things are now at the shelter or how you would like it to be after the consortium's application is live?
>
> **Mary**: I don't think it matters. We are not changing anything with the new system. A pet is a pet.
>
> You: Ok, that makes things easy.

As we can see from our conversations on these first three questions, getting to the answers is rarely straightforward and easy. However, it is much more efficient to ask them at the beginning of the initiative instead of making assumptions early on and having to perform rework later, when changes are time-consuming and expensive.

4. Forward or reverse engineering?

Since we first need to understand how the business works before implementing a software solution, this is a forward engineering project, and we will choose the forward engineering option. This means driven by requirements and, therefore, our terms will be business terms instead of application terms.

5. Operational, analytics, or query?

Since this initiative is about displaying pet information to drive pet adoption, which is query, we will build a query BTM.

6. Who is our audience?

That is, who is going to validate the model and who is going to use it going forward? Mary seems like the best candidate to be the validator. She knows the existing application and processes very well and is vested in ensuring the new initiative succeeds. Potential adopters will be the users of the system.

Step 2: Identify and define the terms

We first focus on the user stories, then determine the detailed queries for each story, and finally sequence these queries in the order they occur. It can be iterative. For example, we might identify the sequence between two queries and realize that a query in the middle is missing that will require modifying or adding a user story. Let's go through each of these three steps.

1. Write user stories

User stories have been around for a long time and are extremely useful for NoSQL modeling. Wikipedia defines a user story as: *...an informal, natural language description of features of a software system.*

The user story provides the scope and overview for the BTM, also known as a query alignment model. A query alignment model accommodates one or more user stories. The purpose of a user story is to capture at a very high level how an initiative will deliver business value. User stories take the structure of the template in Figure 42.

TEMPLATE	COVERS
AS A (STAKEHOLDER)	WHO?
I WANT TO (REQUIREMENT)	WHAT?
SO THAT (MOTIVATION)	WHY?

Figure 42: User story template.

Here are some examples of user stories from tech.gsa.gov:

- As a Content Owner, I want to be able to create product content so that I can provide information and market to customers.

- As an Editor, I want to review content before it is published so that I can ensure it is optimized with correct grammar and tone.

- As a HR Manager, I need to view a candidate's status so that I can manage their application process throughout the recruiting phases.

- As a Marketing Data Analyst, I need to run the Salesforce and Google analytics reports so that I can build the monthly media campaign plans.

To keep our animal shelter example relatively simple, assume our animal shelter and others that are part of the consortium met and determined these are the most popular user stories:

1. As a potential dog adopter, I want to find a particular breed, color, size, and gender, so that I get the type of dog I seek. I want to ensure that the dog's vaccinations are up-to-date.

2. As a potential bird adopter, I want to find a particular breed and color so that I get the type of bird I seek.

3. As a potential cat adopter, I want to find a particular color and gender, so that I get the type of cat I seek.

2. Capture queries

Next, we capture the queries for the one or more user stories within our initiative's scope. While we want to capture multiple user stories to ensure we have a firm grasp of the scope, having just a single user story that drives a NoSQL application is ok. A query starts off with a "verb" and is an action to do something. Some NoSQL database vendors use the phrase "access pattern" instead of query. We will use the term "query" to also encompass "access pattern."

Here are the queries that satisfy our three user stories:

Q1: Only show pets available for adoption.

Q2: Search available dogs by breed, color, size, and gender that have up-to-date vaccinations.

Q3: Search available birds by breed and color.

Q4: Search available cats by color and gender.

Now that we have direction, we can work with the business experts to identify and define the terms within the initiative's scope.

Recall our definition of a term as a noun that represents a collection of business data and is considered both basic and critical to your audience for a particular initiative. A term can fit into one of six categories: who, what, when, where, why, or how. We can use these six categories to create a terms template for capturing the terms on our BTM. See Figure 43.

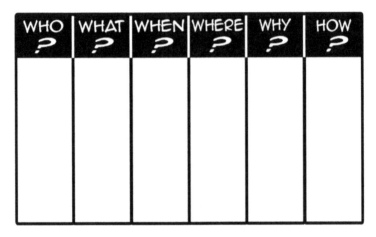

Figure 43: Terms template.

This is a handy brainstorming tool. There is no significance to the numbers. That is, a term written next to #1 is not meant to be more important than a term written next to #2. In addition, you can have more than five terms in a given column, or in some cases, no terms in a given column.

We meet again with Mary, and came up with this completed template in Figure 44, based on our queries.

WHO ?	WHAT ?	WHEN ?	WHERE ?	WHY ?	HOW ?
SURRENDERER	PET	VACCINATION DATE	CRATE	VACCINATE	VACCINATION
ADOPTER	DOG			ADOPT	ADOPTION
	CAT			PROMOTE	PROMOTION
	BIRD				
	BREED				
	GENDER				
	COLOR				
	SIZE				
	IMAGE				

Figure 44: Initially completed template for our animal shelter.

Notice that this is a brainstorming session, and terms might appear on this template but not on the relational BTM. Excluded terms fit into three categories:

- **Too detailed.** Attributes will appear on the LDM and not the BTM. For example, **Vaccination Date** is more detailed than **Pet** and **Breed**.

- **Out of scope.** Brainstorming is a great way to test the scope of the initiative. Often, terms added to the terms template require additional discussions to determine whether they are in scope. For example, **Surrenderer** and **Adopter** we know are out of scope for the animal shelter's initiative.

- **Redundancies**. Why and How can be very similar. For example, the event **Vaccinate** is documented by the **Vaccination**. The event **Adopt** is documented by **Adoption**. Therefore, we may not need both the event and documentation. In this case, we choose the documentation. That is, we choose How instead of Why.

After taking a lunch break, we met again with Mary and refined our terms template, as shown in Figure 45.

WHO ?	WHAT ?	WHEN ?	WHERE ?	WHY ?	HOW ?
~~SURRENDERER~~	PET	~~VACCINATION DATE~~	~~CRATE~~	~~VACCINATE~~	VACCINATION
~~ADOPTER~~	DOG			~~ADOPT~~	~~ADOPTION~~
	CAT			~~PROMOTE~~	~~PROMOTION~~
	BIRD				
	BREED				
	GENDER				
	COLOR				
	SIZE				
	IMAGE				

Figure 45: Refined template for our animal shelter.

We might have a lot of questions during this brainstorming session. It is a great idea to ask questions as they come up. There are three benefits of raising questions:

- **Become known as the detective**. Become comfortable with the level of detective work needed to arrive at a precise set of terms. Look for holes in the definition where ambiguity can sneak in, and ask questions the answers to which will make the definition precise. Consider the question, "Can a pet be of more than one breed?" The answer to this question will refine how the consortium views pets, breeds, and their relationship. A skilled detective remains pragmatic as well, careful to avoid "analysis paralysis." A skilled data modeler must also be pragmatic to ensure the delivery of value to the project team.

- **Uncover hidden terms**. Often the answers to questions lead to more terms on our BTM—terms that we might have missed otherwise. For example, better understanding the relationship between **Vaccination** and **Pet** might lead to more terms on our BTM.

- **Better now than later**. The resulting BTM offers a lot of value, yet the process of getting to that final model is also valuable. Debates and questions challenge people, make them rethink and, in some cases, defend their perspectives. If questions are not raised and answered during the process of building the BTM, the questions will be raised and need to be addressed later on in the lifecycle of the initiative, often in the form of data and process surprises, when changes are time-consuming and expensive. Even simple questions like "Are there other attributes that we could use to describe a pet?" can lead to a healthy debate resulting in a more precise BTM.

Here are definitions for each term:

Pet	A dog, cat, or bird that is ready and available to be adopted. An animal becomes a pet after they have passed certain exams administered by our shelter staff.
Gender	The biological sex of the pet. There are three values that we use at the shelter: • Male • Female • Unknown The unknown value is when we are unsure of the gender.
Size	The size is most relevant for dogs, and there are three values that we assign at the shelter: • Small • Medium • Large Cats and birds are assigned medium, except for kittens which are assigned small and parrots which are large.
Color	The primary shade of the pet's fur, feathers, or coat. Examples of colors include brown, red, gold, cream, and black. If a pet has multiple colors, we either assign a primary color or assign a more general term to encompass multiple colors, such as textured, spotted, or patched.

Breed	From Wikipedia, because this definition applies to our initiative: *A breed is a specific group of domestic animals having homogeneous appearance, homogeneous behavior, and/or other characteristics that distinguish it from other organisms of the same species.*
Vaccina -tion	A shot given to a pet to protect it from disease. Examples of vaccinations are rabies for dogs and cats, and polyomavirus vaccine for birds.
Image	A photograph taken of the pet that will be posted on the website.
Dog	From Wikipedia, because this definition applies to our initiative: *The dog is a domesticated descendant of the wolf. Also called the domestic dog, it is derived from the extinct Pleistocene wolf, and the modern wolf is the dog's nearest living relative. Dogs were the first species to be domesticated by hunter-gatherers over 15,000 years ago before the development of agriculture.*
Cat	From Wikipedia, because this definition applies to our initiative: *The cat is a domestic species of small carnivorous mammal. It is the only domesticated species in the family Felidae and is commonly referred to as the domestic cat or house cat to distinguish it from the wild members of the family.*
Bird	From Wikipedia, because this definition applies to our initiative: *Birds are a group of warm-blooded vertebrates constituting the class Aves, characterized by feathers, toothless beaked jaws, the laying of hard-shelled eggs, a high metabolic rate, a four-chambered heart, and a strong yet lightweight skeleton.*

Step 3: Capture the relationships

Even though this is a query BTM, we can ask the Participation and Existence questions to precisely display the business rules for each relationship. Participation questions determine whether there is a one or a many symbol on the relationship line next to each term. Existence questions determine whether there is a zero (may) or one (must) symbol on the relationship line next to either term.

Working with Mary, we identify these relationships on the model:

- **Pet** can be a **Bird, Cat,** or **Dog.** (Subtyping)
- **Pet** and **Image.**
- **Pet** and **Breed.**
- **Pet** and **Gender.**
- **Pet** and **Color.**
- **Pet** and **Vaccination.**
- **Pet** and **Size.**

Table 5 contains the answers to the Participation and Existence questions for each of these seven relationships (excluding the subtyping relationship).

After translating the answer to each question into the model, we have the animal shelter BTM in Figure 46.

Question	Yes	No
Can a Gender categorize more than one Pet?	✓	
Can a Pet be categorized by more than one Gender?		✓
Can a Gender exist without a Pet?	✓	
Can a Pet exist without a Gender?		✓
Can a Size categorize more than one Pet?	✓	
Can a Pet be categorized by more than one Size?		✓
Can a Size exist without a Pet?	✓	
Can a Pet exist without a Size?		✓
Can a Color describe more than one Pet?	✓	
Can a Pet be described by more than one Color?		✓
Can a Color exist without a Pet?	✓	
Can a Pet exist without a Color?		✓
Can a Pet be described by more than one Breed?	✓	
Can a Breed describe more than one Pet?	✓	
Can a Pet exist without a Breed?		✓
Can a Breed exist without a Pet?	✓	
Can a Pet be given more than one Vaccination?	✓	
Can a Vaccination be given to more than one Pet?	✓	
Can a Pet exist without a Vaccination?	✓	
Can a Vaccination exist without a Pet?	✓	
Can a Pet take more than one Image?	✓	
Can an Image be taken of more than one Pet?	✓	
Can a Pet exist without an Image?		✓
Can an Image exist without a Pet?		✓

Table 5: Answers to the Participation and Existence questions.

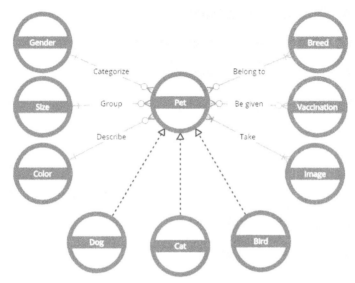

Figure 46: Our animal shelter BTM (showing rules).

These relationships are read as:

- Each **Gender** may categorize many **Pets**.
- Each **Pet** must be categorized by one **Gender**.
- Each **Size** may group many **Pets**.
- Each **Pet** must be grouped by one **Size**.
- Each **Color** may describe many **Pets**.
- Each **Pet** must be described by one **Color**.
- Each **Pet** must belong to many **Breeds**.
- Each **Breed** may be assigned to many **Pets**.
- Each **Pet** may be given many **Vaccinations**.
- Each **Vaccination** may be given to many **Pets**.
- Each **Pet** must take many **Images**.
- Each **Image** must be taken of many **Pets**.
- Each **Pet** may either be a **Dog**, **Cat**, or **Bird**.
- **Dog** is a **Pet**. **Cat** is a **Pet**. **Bird** is a **Pet**.

The answers to the participation and existence questions are context-dependent. That is, the scope of the initiative determines the answers. In this case, because our scope is the subset of the animal shelter's business that will be used as part of this consortium's project, we know at this point that a **Pet** must be described by only one **Color**.

We determined, though, that a Elasticsearch database should be used to answer these queries. You can see how the traditional data model provides value by making us ask the right questions and then providing a powerful communication medium showing the terms and their business rules. Even if we are not implementing our solution in a relational database, this BTM provides value.

> *Build a relational data model even though the solution is in a NoSQL database such as Elasticsearch, if you feel there can be value. That is, if you feel there is value in explaining the terms with precision along with their business rules, build the relational BTM. If you feel there is value in organizing the attributes into sets using normalization, build the relational LDM. It will help you organize your thoughts and provide you with a very effective communication tool.*

Our end goal, though, is to create an Elasticsearch database. Therefore, we need a query BTM. So we need to determine the order in which someone would run the queries.

Graphing the sequence of queries leads to the query BTM. The query BTM is a numbered list of all queries necessary to deliver the user stories within the initiative's scope. The model also shows a sequence or dependency among the queries. The query BTM for our five queries would look like what appears in Figure 47.

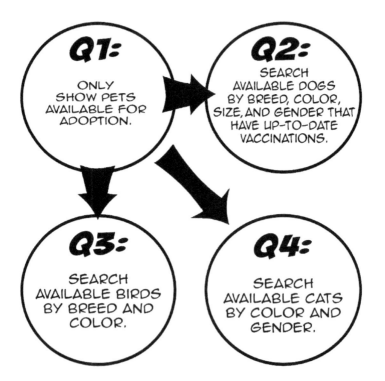

Figure 47: Our animal shelter BTM (showing queries).

All of the queries depend on the first query. That is, we first need to filter by animal type.

Step 4: Determine the visual

Someone will need to review your work and use your model as input for future deliverables such as software development, so deciding on the most useful visual is an important step. After getting an answer to Strategic Question #4, *Who is our audience?*, we know that Mary will be our validator.

There are many different ways of displaying the BTM. Factors include the technical competence of the audience and the existing tools environment.

However, it would be helpful to know which data modeling notations and data modeling tools are currently being used within the organization. If the audience is familiar with a particular data modeling notation—such as Information Engineering (IE), which we have been using throughout this book—that is the notation we should use. If the audience is familiar with a particular data modeling tool, such as IDERA's ER/Studio, erwin DM, or Hackolade Studio, and that data modeling tool uses a different notation, we should use that tool with that notation to create the BTM.

Luckily, the two BTMs we created, one for rules and one for queries, are very intuitive, so there is a very good chance our models will be well-understood by the audience.

Step 5: Review and confirm

Previously we identified the person or group responsible for validating the model. Now we need to show them the model and make sure it is correct. Often at this stage, after reviewing the model, we make some changes and then show them the model again. This iterative cycle continues until the validator approves the model.

Three tips

1. **Organization**. The steps you went through in building this "model" are the same steps we go through in building any model. It is all about organizing information. Data modelers are fantastic organizers. We take the chaotic real world and show it in a precise form, creating powerful communication tools.

2. **80/20 Rule.** Don't go for perfection. Too many requirements meetings end with unfulfilled goals by spending too much time discussing a minute particular issue. After a few minutes of discussion, if you feel the issue's discussion may take up too much time and not lead to a resolution, document the issue and keep going. You will find that for modeling to work well with Agile and other iterative approaches, you may have to forego perfection and sometimes even completion. Much better to document the unanswered

questions and issues and keep going. Much better to deliver something imperfect yet still very valuable than deliver nothing. You will find that you can get the data model about 80% complete in 20% of the time. One of your deliverables will be a document containing unanswered questions and unresolved issues. Once all of these issues and questions are resolved, which will take about 80% of your time to complete, the model will be 100% complete.

3. **Diplomat.** As William Kent said in **Data and Reality** (1978), *so, once again, if we are going to have a database about books, before we can know what one representative stands for, we had better have a consensus among all users as to what "one book" is.* Invest time trying to get consensus on terms before building a solution. Imagine someone querying on pets without having a clear definition of what a pet is.

Three takeaways

1. Six strategic questions must be asked before you begin any project (Step 1). These questions are a prerequisite to the success of any initiative because they ensure we choose the right terms for our BTM. Next, identify all terms within the scope of the initiative (Step 2). Make sure each term is clearly and completely defined. Then

determine how these terms are related (Step 3). Often, you will need to go back to Step 2 at this point, because in capturing relationships, you may come up with new terms. Next, determine the most beneficial visual for your audience (Step 4). Consider the visual that would resonate best with those needing to review and use your BTM. As a final step, seek approval of your BTM (Step 5). Often at this point, there are additional changes to the model, and we cycle through these steps until the model is accepted.

2. Create a relational BTM in addition to a query BTM if you feel there would be value in capturing and explaining the participation and existence rules.

3. Never underestimate the value of precise and complete definitions.

CHAPTER 2

Refine

This chapter will explain the data modeling refine phase. We explain the purpose of refine, refine the model for our animal shelter case study, and then walk through the refine approach. We end the chapter with three tips and three takeaways.

Purpose

The purpose of the refinement stage is to create the logical data model (LDM) based on our common business vocabulary defined during the align stage. Refine is how the modeler captures the business requirements without complicating the model with implementation concerns, such as software and hardware.

The shelter's Logical Data Model (LDM) uses the common business language from the BTM to precisely define the business requirements. The LDM is fully-attributed yet independent of technology. We build the relational LDM by normalizing, covered in Chapter 1. Figure 48 contains the shelter's relational LDM.

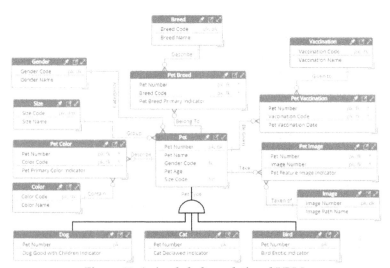

Figure 48: Animal shelter relational LDM.

This model does not change based on requirements. Therefore, we can use it as the starting point model for all queries. Let's briefly walk through the model. The shelter identifies each **Pet** with a **Pet Number**, which is a unique counter assigned to the **Pet** the day the **Pet** arrives. Also entered at this time are the pet's name (**Pet Name**) and age (**Pet Age**). If the **Pet** does not have a name, it is given one by the shelter employee entering the pet's information. If the age is unknown, it is estimated by the shelter employee entering the pet's information. If the **Pet** is a **Dog**, the shelter employee entering the information performs a few assessments to determine whether the Dog is good with children (**Dog Good With Children Indicator**). If the **Pet** is a **Cat**, the shelter employee determines whether the **Cat** has been declawed (**Cat Declawed Indicator**). If the Pet is a **Bird**, the shelter employee enters whether it is an exotic bird such as a parrot (**Bird Exotic Indicator**).

Approach

The refine stage is all about determining the business requirements for the initiative. The end goal is a logical data model which captures the attributes and relationships needed to answer the queries. The steps to complete appear in Figure 49.

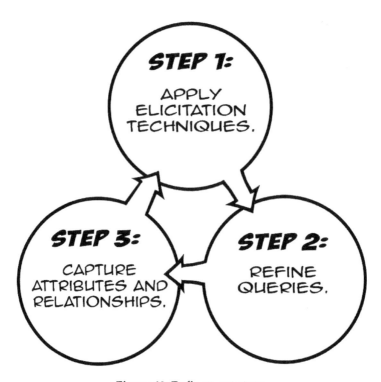

Figure 49: Refinement steps.

Similar to determining the more detailed structures in a traditional logical data model, we determine the more detailed structures needed to deliver the queries during the refinement stage. You can therefore call the query LDM a query refinement model if you prefer. The query refinement model is all about discovery and captures the answers to the queries that reveal insights into a business process.

Step 1: Apply elicitation techniques

This is where we interact with the business stakeholders to identify the attributes and relationships needed to answer the queries. We keep refining, usually until we run out of time. Techniques we can use include interviewing, artifact analysis (studying existing or proposed business or technical documents), job shadowing (watching someone work), and prototyping. You can use any combination of these techniques to obtain the attributes and relationships to answer the queries. Often these techniques are used within an Agile framework. You choose which techniques to use based on your starting point and the needs of the stakeholders. For example, if a stakeholder says, "I don't know what I want, but I'll know when I see it," building a prototype might be the best approach.

Analyze workloads

An important part of this exercise is to identify, quantify, and qualify the workload.

You need to identify each operation as either a read or a write operation and understand the read-to-write ratio. Make a list of all Create, Read, Update, and Delete (CRUD) operations, and take the time to go through the exercise of drawing wireframes of screens and reports, and of assembling workflow diagrams. Thinking these through and validating them with subject matter experts will inevitably reveal facts you might have previously overlooked.

Elasticsearch uses sharding (partitioning) for scalability. The data is split into multiple partitions and stored separately. These partitions are referred to as shards. We can distribute the shards across multiple machines that can handle requests in parallel, improving the overall performance. In addition to that, more machines can be added if the load increases. The data stored in indices is split into primary shards so that each document in an index belongs to exactly one primary shard.

Elasticsearch also uses replication, which is storing multiple copies of the same data separately. Replicas can be found on multiple machines, providing a backup copy of the data if something goes wrong with a machine. Replicas can also execute read requests together, which helps system load-sharing. These replicas, called replica shards, are simply copies of the primary shard.

Before starting our design exercise and looking into performance metrics which influence the design, we need to look a bit further into how Elasticsearch operates. A cluster is made up of one or more nodes, as illustrated in Figure 50.

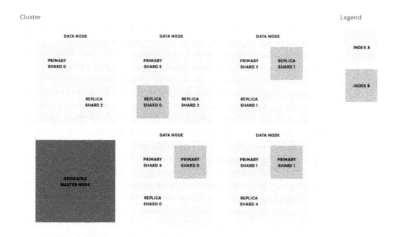

Figure 50: Elasticsearch cluster.[4]

There are three common types of nodes:

- **Primary-eligible node:** By default, every node is primary-eligible. A cluster automatically selects a primary node from all the ones that are eligible. If the primary node fails, another eligible node will be designated as primary. The primary nodes coordinate cluster tasks such as deleting or creating indices, as well as performing shard distribution.

- **Data node:** By default, every node is also a data node responsible for storing data in shards. These perform operations related to indexing, searching, and aggregating data.

---

[4] https://solutionhacker.com/elasticsearch-architecture-overview/.

- **Client node:** This node performs load balancing, which helps route indexing and search requests. It helps ease the search workload to aid data and primary-eligible nodes remain dedicated to their specific functions. Client nodes are not always necessary if data nodes can handle the request routing on their own.

Data is stored in indices, as mentioned earlier. An Elasticsearch index is a storage entity, similar to a collection in MongoDB or a table in RDBMS. Each index contains a set of related documents in JSON format. A key concept in Elasticsearch is the inverted index, which lists every distinct word in a given document and identifies each document in which this word occurs. We need to consider how to define these indices. An index is stored across one or many primary shards and zero or many replica shards.

When creating an index, we can specify the number of primary shards and the number of replica shards per primary shard. Choose the index carefully, as the number of primary shards cannot be changed.

For read and write operations, also known as search and indexing, respectively, in Elasticsearch, we need to consider some key performance metrics for proper workload analysis.

Search requests are similar to read requests in a traditional database. Search requests have two main phases, query and fetch, which lead to three key search performance metrics:

- **Query Load:** Number of requests currently in progress which gives an idea of how many requests the cluster is dealing with at a specific point in time. Setting up alerts on random spikes and dips in the query load is possible to get to underlying problems.

- **Query Latency:** Monitoring tools can calculate the average query latency by using the total number of queries and total elapsed time. Set up alerts if the latency exceeds a specified threshold.

- **Fetch Latency:** The fetch phase of searching should take much less time than the querying phase. If this metric is always increasing, this could mean you need to enrich the documents, or there could be a memory issue.

Indexing requests are similar to write requests in a traditional database. When information is changed in an index, each shard of the index is updated via two processes: refresh and flush. By default, Elasticsearch refreshes indices every second. However, this interval can be altered. Flushing an index ensures that data stored in the transaction log is permanently stored in the Lucene index (Apache

Lucene is the base of Elasticsearch). There are two key indexing performance metrics:

- **Index Latency:** Monitoring tools can calculate the indexing latency using the index total and index time metrics. If there are a large number of documents, choose to optimize for indexing performance over search performance.

- **Flush Latency:** Data is not persisted to disk until a flush is completed, so this metric may help resolve issues preventing you from adding new information to your index.

For write operations, you want to know how long to hold data, the frequency by which data is transmitted to the system, average document size, retention, and durability. Start your design exercise with the most critical operation and work your way down the list.

For read operations, you also want to document the patterns and required freshness of the data, taking into account eventual consistency and read latency. Data freshness is related to replication time if you read from a secondary, or to the acceptable time for a piece of data derived from other pieces. It defines how fast written data must be accessible for read operations: immediately (data consistent at all times), within ten milliseconds, within one second, within one minute, within one hour, or within one day. For example, reading the top reviews associated with a product, which are cached in the product document, may have a tolerated one-day freshness. Read latency is specified in milliseconds, where p95 and p99 values represent the 95th and 99th percentile values. A read latency p95 value of 100ms means 95 out of 100 requests took 100ms or less to complete.

This information helps validate the choice of design pattern (described later in the book), orients the necessary indexes, and impacts the sizing and provisioning of the hardware, hence the budget for the project. Different data modeling patterns impact read performance, number of write operations, cost of indexes, etc. So you may have to make compromises and sometimes balance contradictory needs.

You may use a spreadsheet or any other method to document the results of your workload analysis, based on the example in Figure 51, which is built into Hackolade Studio for Elasticsearch. When considering schema evolution later in the lifecycle, you will be able to review the values originally recorded, as reality might be very different than what was originally estimated. Document the query predicates with the specific expression and parameters used to determine which documents should be retrieved. A couple of other data points in the form in Figure 51 deserve some clarification.

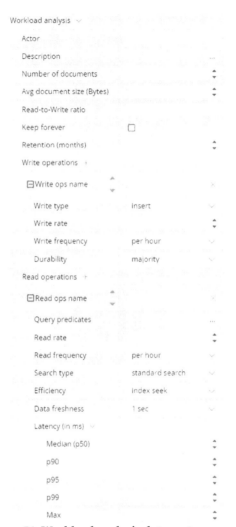

Figure 51: Workload analysis data capture screen.

The Search type property allows you to indicate the type of index to define for improving the performance of your queries:

- **Standard search**: with this value, we mark queries based on one or more fields in the document, possibly combined in the aggregation pipeline;

- **Geospatial query**: allows for efficient retrieval of documents based on their geographic location or proximity to a specific point for applications with location-based searches or geospatial analysis;

- **Text search**: enables the search for text within text-indexed fields when efficient and relevance-based searches across large volumes of text-based data are required;

The shape of your document and the definition of the index for the collection directly impact the efficiency of your queries. The following values are listed from most efficient to least efficient:

- **Covered query**: the index contains all the queried fields and the necessary data to fulfill the query, eliminating the need for fetching documents from the collection itself;

- **Index seek**: the index quickly locates and retrieves specific documents based on the specified query criteria, minimizing the number of scanned documents;

- **Index scan**: focuses on seeking a specific document or range of documents based on the query predicates, efficiently narrowing down the search;

- **Collection scan**: when no indexes can be used to efficiently filter or locate the desired data, this pattern is resource-intensive and time-consuming, especially for large collections with a significant number of documents.

Quantify relationships

Since the advent of entity relationship diagrams, we restricted ourselves to using zero, one, and many as the different cardinalities of relationships.

This may have been appropriate for the longest time; however, the world has changed. Datasets are a few orders of magnitude larger than they were a few years ago. Not understanding that a relationship's "many" side may refer to thousands or millions of objects and trying to embed, pull, or join these objects may not work well for most applications. Because these humongous relationships are more frequent than before, we suggest quantifying them not just with "many" but with actual numbers. For example, instead of using [0, M] to say that an object can be linked to zero-to-many objects, we should try to quantify these numbers whenever possible. For example, a product may have [0, 1000] reviews. This is more telling. Writing 1000 down makes us think about pagination and possibly limiting the number of reviews on a product when it reaches the maximum value.

To increase our knowledge about the relationship, we can add an optional "most likely" or "median" value. For example, [0, 20, 1000] is more descriptive by telling us that a product may have 0 to 1000 reviews with a median of 20. If we create our model using Hackolade Studio, the arrays in a document can be modeled with the cardinalities in Figure 52.

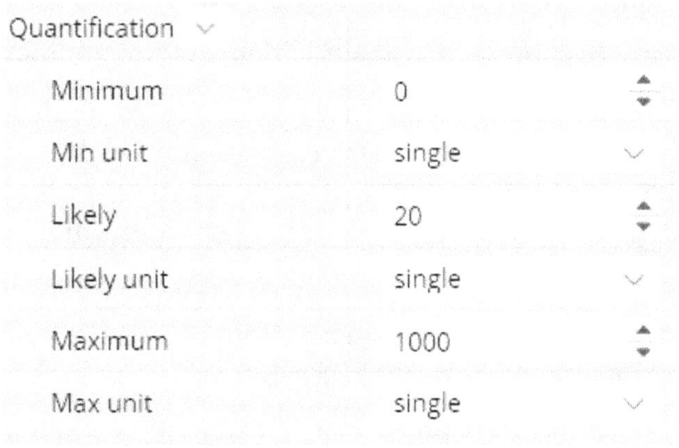

Quantification ⌄		
Minimum	0	⬍
Min unit	single	⌄
Likely	20	⬍
Likely unit	single	⌄
Maximum	1000	⬍
Max unit	single	⌄

Figure 52: Cardinalities.

And yes, we will get these numbers wrong, especially at the beginning. However, we should get the order of magnitude right. If we don't get it right, it is a red flag to review the model. Maybe a piece of information should not be embedded but referenced instead.

Step 2: Refine queries

The refinement process is iterative, and we keep refining, again, usually until we run out of time.

Step 3: Capture attributes and relationships

Ideally, because of the hierarchical nature of document (and also key-value) databases, we should strive to answer one or more queries with a single structure. Although this might seem "anti-normalization, "one structure organized to a particular query is much faster and simpler than connecting multiple structures. The logical data model contains the attributes and related structures needed for each of the queries identified in the query refinement model.

Using artifact analysis, we can start with the animal shelter's logical and use this model as a good way to capture the attributes and relationships within our scope. Based on the queries, quite a few of our concepts are not directly needed for search or filtering, and so they can become additional descriptive attributes on the **Pet** entity.

For example, no critical queries involved vaccinations. Therefore, we can simplify this model subset from the model in Figure 53 to the model in Figure 54.

Figure 53: Normalized model subset.

Figure 54: Denormalized model subset.

This example illustrates how traditional RDBMS models differ from NoSQL. On our original logical model, it was important to communicate that a **Pet** can receive many **Vaccinations** and a **Vaccination** can be given to many **Pets**. In NoSQL, however, since there were no queries needing to filter or search by vaccination, the vaccination attributes just became other descriptive attributes of **Pet**. The **Vaccination Code** and **Vaccination Name** attributes are now a nested array within **Pet**. So, for example, if Spot the Dog had five vaccinations, they would all be listed within Spot's record (or *document* to use Elasticsearch terminology). Following this same logic, the pet's colors and images also become nested arrays, as shown in Figure 55. The nested data type in Elasticsearch is a specialized version of the object data type. If, in the future, vaccination needs to be queried, this array of objects can be indexed in a way so that they can be queried independently in Elasticsearch.

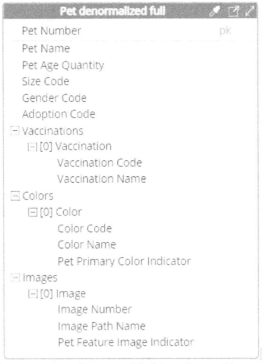

Figure 55: Nested arrays added for color and images.

In addition, to help with querying, we need to create a **Pet Type** structure instead of the subtypes, **Dog**, **Cat**, and **Bird**. After determining the available pets for adoption, we need to distinguish whether the **Pet** is a **Dog**, **Cat**, or **Bird**. Our model would now look like what appears in Figure 56. When subtyping, the implications on indexing in Elasticsearch need to be considered. Sometimes, you might be better off denormalizing all the data into the child documents rather than having a parent/child concept. This might not always be practical as there might be too much data in the parent documents to duplicate into the child document. Another option is to place child documents within the parent document. A potential drawback is that adding a child document will require reindexing of the entire document.

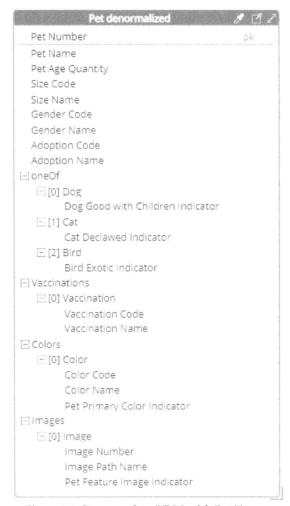

Figure 56: Our complete LDM with Pet Type.

In addition to the denormalization seen before, this example illustrates the polymorphic nature of Elasticsearch's document model as an alternative to the inheritance tables of relational databases. This single schema describes and can validate different document types for dogs, cats, and birds, in addition to the common structure. Relational subtyping is accomplished here with the oneOf choice, which allows multiple subschemas.

Elasticsearch provides two options to help with avoiding reindexing. The first is creating a nested document or query. This allows you to have a parent/child relationship between documents. However, when indexing the child, you must provide the id of the parent. The second is using a has_child filter, which selects parent documents with at least one child satisfying a certain query. The main benefit of using these hierarchical relationships is that a child is always indexed in the same shard as its parent, so has_child doesn't have to rely on confusing cross-shard operations. As mentioned earlier, these shards are crucial to facilitate distribution and scalability.

Junction tables found in relational models are replaced by arrays of subobjects, the array data type allowing for an ordered list of items.

Three tips

1. **Access patterns:** the query-driven approach is critical to leverage the benefits of NoSQL when creating an LDM. Don't be tempted by old normalization habits unless the workload analysis reveals relationship cardinality that warrants normalization. Keep in mind

the key concepts of hierarchies and nesting when building the model.

2. **Aggregates:** keep together what belongs together! A nested structure in a single document can ensure atomicity and consistency of inserts, updates, and queries without expensive joins. It is also beneficial for developers who are used to working with objects, and it is easier to understand for humans.

3. **It is easier to normalize a denormalized structure than the opposite**: a normalized LDM is not technology-agnostic if it includes supertypes/subtypes or junction tables. Or it is "technology-agnostic" only if your physical targets are exclusively relational and don't include NoSQL. A denormalized LDM, on the other hand, can be easily normalized for relational physical targets by a good data modeling tool, while providing denormalized structures based on the access patterns identified earlier. However, the focus still needs to be kept on building a data model that correctly captures business concepts and relationships. At this point, technology considerations are secondary.

Three takeaways

1. The purpose of the refinement stage is to create the logical data model (LDM) based on our common

business vocabulary, defined for our initiative during the align stage. Refine is how the modeler captures the business requirements without complicating the model with implementation concerns, such as software and hardware. Hence, it is important to understand when to choose Elasticsearch over RDBMS and other NoSQL databases, and how Elasticsearch operates.

2. An LDM is typically fully-attributed yet independent of technology. But this strict definition is being challenged nowadays because technology targets can be so different in nature: relational databases, the different families of NoSQL, storage formats for data lakes, pub/sub pipelines, APIs, etc. Experiment with different designs before finalizing one. This especially applies to the concepts of nesting and subtyping.

3. It used to be, with relational databases, that you wanted to design a structure that could handle any possible future query down the road. With NoSQL, you want to design schemas that are specific, not only for an application, but for each access pattern (write or read) in that application.

CHAPTER 3

Design

This chapter will explain the data modeling design phase. We explain the purpose of design, design the model for our animal shelter case study, and then walk through the design approach. We end the chapter with three tips and three takeaways.

Purpose

The purpose of the design stage is to create the physical data model (PDM) based on the business requirements defined on our logical data model. Design is how the modeler captures the technical requirements without compromising the business requirements yet accommodating the initiative's software and technology needs used for the initiative.

The design stage is also where we accommodate history. We modify our structures to capture how data changes over time. For example, the Design stage would allow us to keep track of not just the most recent name for a pet, but also the original. For example, the animal shelter changes a pet's name from Sparky to Daisy. Our design could store the original pet name and the most current, so we would know Daisy's original name was Sparky. Although this is not a book on temporal data or modeling approaches that gracefully allow for storing high data volatility or varying history requirements, such as the Data Vault,[5] you would need to consider such factors in the Design stage.

Figure 57 shows the Physical Data Model (PDM) of the animal shelter's Microsoft Access database design.

------

[5] For more on the data vault, read John Giles' *The Elephant in the Fridge*.

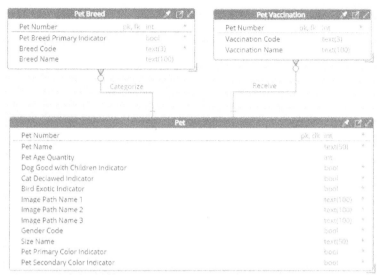

Figure 57: PDM of the shelter's Access database.

Note that the PDM includes formatting and nullability. Also, this model is heavily denormalized. For example:

- Although the logical communicates that a **Pet** can have any number of images, their design only allows up to three images for each **Pet**. The shelter uses **Image_Path_Name_1** for the featured image.

- Notice how the decode entities from the logical have been addressed. The one-to-many relationships are denormalized into **Pet**. **Gender_Name** is not needed because everyone knows the codes. People are not familiar with **Size_Code** so only **Size_Name** is stored. **Breed** has been denormalized into **Pet_Breed**. It is common for decode entities to be modeled in different ways on the physical, depending on the requirements.

- **Vaccination** has been denormalized into **Pet_Vaccination**.

For Elasticsearch, it would look more like the model in Figure 58.

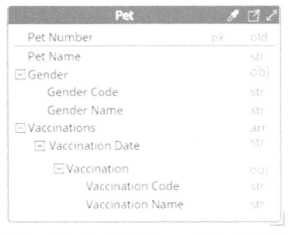

Figure 58: If modeling the shelter's Access database in Elasticsearch.

Approach

The design stage is all about developing the database-specific design for the initiative. The end goal is the query PDM, which we can also call the *query design model*. For our animal shelter initiative, this model captures the Elasticsearch design and JSON interchange format for the initiative. The steps to complete appear in Figure 59.

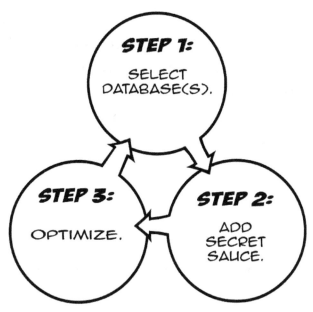

Figure 59: Design steps.

Step 1: Select database(s)

We now know enough to decide which database would be ideal for the application. Sometimes we might choose more than one database if we feel it would be the best architecture for the application. In the case of Elasticsearch, we know that they are using an ODBC connector to ingest data from MS Access and Elasticsearch as a data store. Additionally, Elasticsearch can be schema-less, so indexing in documents can occur without explicit specification of the handling of each field within a document. With the built-in dynamic mapping functionality, which you can enable, you can automatically detect and add new fields to indices.

Step 2: Add secret sauce

Although document NoSQL databases can be quite similar, each database has something special to consider during design. For example, for Elasticsearch, we would consider where to use their secret sauce, such as Elasticsearch-specific functionality like the following:

- Indexing
- Schema-less
- Clustering
- Sharding
- Cross-cluster and cross-data center replication
- Automatic node recovery
- Automatic data rebalancing
- DSL, SQL and EQL querying
- ABAC and RBAC for access control
- Snapshot lifecycle management
- Data storage flexibility (multiple supported data types, document store, full-text search, time series, geospatial)
- Built-in ingestion and enrichment APIs.

Inner objects vs. parent/child vs. nesting

Inner objects

When you model for Elasticsearch, inner objects (embedding) are commonly seen for any type of relationship. Choosing whether to embed a document within another as an inner object or create a nested structure will lead to a difference in functionality. Making the right decision for each relationship will give you the best model among all possible models.

In a relational database model, one-to-one relationships tend to be embedded. The two pieces of information live in the same row. In the case of one-to-many or many-to-many relationships, the two pieces of information are divided into different rows in different tables. With Elasticsearch, embedding a one-to-one relationship means putting the two pieces of information in the same document. You could also opt to use a subdocument to group related information, such as the components of an address:

```
// A one-to-one relationship within a subdocument
{
    "_id": "dog19370824",
    "name": "Champ",
    "address": {
        "street": "1600 Pennsylvania Avenue NW",
        "city": "Washington",
        "state": "DC",
        "zip": "20500",
        "country": "USA",
    }
}
```

You embed a one-to-many relationship with an array or a dictionary. An array is the document construct to express a one-to-many relationship in the document model.

```
// a Pet document with embedded Pet comments
{
  "_id": "dog19370824",
  "name": "Fanny",
  "comments": [ {
      "name": "Daniel Coupal",
      "text": "Fanny is the sweetest dog ever!"
    }, {
      "name": "Steve Hoberman",
      "text": "Fanny loved my daughter's brownies."
    } ]
}
```

For a many-to-many relationship, we also use an array or a dictionary. It is important to note that embedding this type of relationship may introduce data duplication. Data duplication is not necessarily bad for your model; however, we want to highlight the difference with embedding a one-to-many relationship where it does not introduce denormalization or data duplication in contrast with the many-to-many relationship.

Parent/child types

We reference another document by using a scalar if the relationship is a "one" or with an array of "references" if the relationship is a "many." The parent document has its own mapping, and the children have their own mapping outside the parent, with a special parent property set. This allows for a looser coupling and for users to write more powerful queries. References can be unidirectional or bi-directional. Using the example of Pets and related comments, we can describe the relationship as: "A Pet may have many comments" and "A comment must be associated with a Pet," getting different alternatives to express the references as illustrated in the following examples. Example of references from the parent's document:

```
// References from the parent document to the child
documents using an array
//
// a Pet document with references to Comment
documents
{
    "_id": "dog19370824",
    "name": "Fanny",
    "comments": [
        "comment101",
        "comment102"
    ]
}
// referenced Comment documents
{
    "_id": "comment01",
    "name": "Daniel Coupal",
    "text": "Fanny is the sweetest dog ever!"
},
{
    "_id": "comment102",
    "name": "Steve Hoberman",
    "text": "Fanny loved my daughter's brownies."
}
```

Examples of references from the children's documents:

```
// References from a child document to the parent
document
//
// a Pet document
{
```

```
    "_id": "dog19370824",
    "name": "Fanny
}
// Comment documents with reference to the parent
document
{
    "_id": "comment01",
    "dog": "dog19370824",
    "name": "Daniel Coupal",
    "text": "Fanny is the sweetest dog ever!"
},
{
    "_id": "comment102",
    "dog": "dog19370824",
    "name": "Steve Hoberman",
    "text": "Fanny loved my daughter's brownies."
}
```

Example of bi-directional references:

```
// References from the parent document to the child
documents and vice-versa
//
// a Pet document with references to Comment
documents
{
    "_id": "dog19370824",
    "name": "Fanny",
    "comments": [
        "comment101",
        "comment102"
    ]
}

// referenced Comment documents with reference to the
parent document
{
    "_id": "comment01",
    "dog": "dog19370824",
    "name": "Daniel Coupal",
```

```
    "text": "Fanny is the sweetest dog ever!"
},
{

    "_id": "comment102",
    "dog": "dog19370824",
    "name": "Steve Hoberman",
    "text": "Fanny loved my daughter's brownies."

}
```

Note that a relational model would usually not have an array of "pets." Joins in relational databases support scalar values, so references are not implemented in both directions. With Elasticsearch, only use the references on the side from which you want to access the other objects. Maintaining bidirectional references is more expensive to manage. To summarize referencing, use a scalar to reference a "one" and an array to reference a "many." Add the references in the main objects from which you will query the data.

Nesting

As an alternative to inner objects, Elasticsearch also provides nested types. Nested types look identical to inner objects but provide some additional functionality as well as some limitations. For the Elasticsearch mapping, nested data types need to be explicitly declared, unlike inner objects that are detected automatically.

Rules and guidelines to choose between inner objects, referencing, and nesting

Let's look into the functionality difference between nesting and inner objects. The problem with inner objects is that each nested object or document is not treated as a single component of the parent document. Instead, they are merged with other inner objects, inheriting the same properties. For nested objects, Elasticsearch manages them internally to show the hierarchy. When you create a nested document, the root and nested objects are indexed separately and then internally related. However, both documents are stored in the same shard, minimally, if at all, affecting read performance.

Using nested objects does have some disadvantages. You can only query nested documents using a special nested query. Additionally, when a document is required to be updated, even a single field, the entire document which contains the nested object will need to be reindexed.

To decide which model to use between inner objects (embedding) and parent/child type (referencing), the main rules are "what is used together in the application is stored together in the database" and "prefer embedding over referencing." Let's explain these two main rules.

Keep everything that is used together in the application together in the database to avoid doing many joins or reads. Joins are costly in terms of CPU and I/O access. Avoiding joins gives much better performance. If each occurrence of the essential query goes from doing three reads and two joins to only one read where the three pieces are embedded, you may have just slashed your hardware requirements by a factor of three.

As you keep what you need together, you may want to avoid bloating the document by excluding unnecessary information. The reason is that reading this document will take up more space in memory, limiting the number of documents you can keep in memory at a given time.

Our second main rule asks that we prefer embedding to referencing. The main reason is that complete objects are usually more straightforward for your application, simpler to archive, and do not require transactions to be updated atomically. In other words, you choose simplicity over complexity by embedding over referencing.

With these two rules in mind, let's look at additional guidelines to help us decide between embedding or referencing. To illustrate the guidelines, we will use an example of a financial application where we have a relationship between people and credit cards. The application is developed by a bank subject to all kinds of financial regulations. Based on the questions we saw earlier in the book, we establish that this is a one-to-many relationship that reads, "a person may have many credit cards" and "a card must be owned by a person." And because our system is making requests about people more than cards, the primary entity of that relationship is the person, not the card. Table 6 below lists the additional guidelines.

The first guideline is "Simplicity." This is directly related to our rule in favor of embedding. The related question is: Would keeping the pieces of information together lead to a simpler data model and code? In our example, having one object in the code for a person with their credit cards gives us a simpler code.

The second guideline is "Go Together." The related question is: Do the pieces of information have a "has-a," "contains," or similar relationship? Here we try to understand the dependence of one piece of information on the other. A person "has-a" credit card, so let's answer 'yes.'

The third guideline is "Query Atomicity." The related question is: Does the application query the pieces of information together? Again, we usually want to load the person's info with the credit cards together in the application, so let's again answer 'yes.'

The fourth guideline is "Update Complexity." The related question is: Are the pieces of information updated together? Not really. We will probably add credit cards without modifying the person's information.

Guideline Name	Question	Embed (Inner Object)	Reference (Parent/Child)
Simplicity	Would keeping the pieces of information together lead to a simpler data model and code?	Yes	
Go Together	Do the pieces of information have a "has-a," "contains," or similar relationship?	Yes	
Query Atomicity	Does the application query the pieces of information together?	Yes	
Update Complexity	Are the pieces of information updated together?	Yes	
Archival	Should the pieces of information be archived at the same time?	Yes	
Cardinality	Is there a high cardinality (current or growing) in a "many" side of the relationship?	No	Yes
Data Duplication	Would data duplication be too complicated to manage and undesired?	No	Yes
Document Size	Would the combined size of the pieces of information take too much memory or transfer bandwidth for the application?	No	Yes
Document Growth	Would the embedded piece grow without bound?	No	Yes
Workload	Are the pieces of information written at different times in a write-heavy workload?		Yes
Individuality	For the children's side of the relationship, can the pieces exist by themselves without a parent?		Yes

Table 6: Embed versus reference guidelines.

Let's pause here. We answered 'yes' three times, leading to choosing 'embedding.' But what happens when we answer 'no'? For the first four rules, a 'no' has no impact. In other words, answering 'no' does not favor 'embedding,' but it also does not tell us we should 'reference.'

The fifth guideline is "Archival." The related question is: Should the pieces of information be archived at the same time? As in our example, this question is only relevant if the system must archive data for regulatory reasons. This guideline is related to the archive schema design pattern we describe later in the book. The essence is that it is easier to archive a single document with all the information in it than a bunch of smaller pieces that would need to be reattached or joined together in the future when looking at the archived information. It is a 'yes.' When a user account is deactivated, we want the card information at that time to also be archived.

The sixth guideline is "Cardinality." The related question is: Is there a high cardinality (current or growing) in the "many" side of the relationship? No person should have a few hundred or a thousand cards. This guideline does not just favor "referencing" in the affirmative. It favors "embedding" in the negative. This reflects the bias we have toward preferring "embedding." If the answer is 'yes,' we want to avoid embedding large arrays. These large arrays make for large documents, and by experience, we know that usually, the information in large arrays is not entirely needed all the time with the base document.

The seventh guideline is "Data Duplication." The related question is: Would data duplication be too complicated to manage and undesired? A one-to-many relationship does not generate data duplication, so we have a 'no' to this question.

The eighth guideline is "Document Size." The related question is: Would the combined size of the pieces of information take too much memory or transfer bandwidth for the application? This is related to the large arrays question, as most big documents contain such large arrays. But here, we want to go further. The document must only be considered 'big' by the consuming application. If it is a mobile application, we are likely more conscious about how much data is transferred. For our example, the total size should be relatively small, even for our mobile applications.

The ninth guideline is "Document Growth." The related question is: Would the embedded piece grow without bound? This question is also related to the document size. However, it also factors in the impact of often updating the same document by adding new elements in arrays. Keeping the information in different documents will make for smaller write operations. In our example, the documents would have little growth over time.

The tenth guideline is "Workload." The related question is: Are the pieces of information written at different times in a write-heavy workload? A write-heavy workload will benefit from writing to different documents and avoiding the contention of writing to the same documents often. The example would be a write-heavy workload only if we produce thousands of cards every second.

The eleventh guideline is "Individuality." The related question is: For the children's side of the relationship, can the pieces exist by themselves without a parent? For our example, let's say 'no.' A card must have an owner printed on it before we add it to the system. If the card could exist without an owner, then embedding the card into a person would cause an issue when we delete the owner, and the card must continue to exist. Relationships, where both sides may exist alone, are better modeled with separate documents.

Tallying the results, it is clear that we should embed the credit cards with the person. If we had answers for both "embedding" and "referencing," we would consider the priority of each guideline regarding our application requirements.

In the case of ambiguity between "embedding" and "referencing," it would make this relationship a good candidate to apply a schema design pattern, which we will discuss later.

Guideline Name	Question	Embed (Inner Object)	Reference (Parent/ Child)
Simplicity	Would keeping the pieces of information together lead to a simpler data model and code?	Yes	
Go Together	Do the pieces of information have a "has-a," "contains," or similar relationship?	Yes	
Query Atomicity	Does the application query the pieces of information together?	Yes	
Update Complexity	Are the pieces of information updated together?	Yes	
Archival	Should the pieces of information be archived at the same time?	Yes	
Cardinality	Is there a high cardinality (current or growing) in a "many" side of the relationship?	No	Yes
Data Duplication	Would data duplication be too complicated to manage and undesired?	No	Yes
Document Size	Would the combined size of the pieces of information take too much memory or transfer bandwidth for the application?	No	Yes
Document Growth	Would the embedded piece grow without bound?	No	Yes
Workload	Are the pieces of information written at different times in a write-heavy workload?		Yes
Individuality	For the children's side of the relationship, can the pieces exist by themselves without a parent?		Yes

Table 7: Example of choosing between embedding and referencing.

Schema design approaches

Our role with this book is to make you aware of all of the possibilities, cover the pros and cons, and share use cases. This should inspire readers as they design their schemas. It is a toolbox. Then it is up to the reader to choose the most appropriate tool for their use cases. When modeling data in an index in Elasticsearch, there are four general patterns: application side joins, denormalization, parent-child, and nested objects. Each of these approaches has its pros and cons, which are context-dependent.

Application side joins

Application side joins are fairly intuitive if one is familiar with relational databases. There are two tables and often the primary key in one table is used as a foreign key in the second table. For example, think of a user and order table. We have userID in the order table as a foreign key to the primary key in the user table. We can easily retrieve all orders for a single user by joining the two tables together. We can create two indices, one for each table, and we can query across the indices. The advantages of this method are that the data is normalized and each index can scale separately based on their individual query requirements and data volumes. This works very well when there are a small number of documents. However, when there are many documents, the disadvantage is that additional queries need to run to join documents during a search, leading to a performance loss. Figure 58 shows our Pet example through an application side join. There are three indices with types within each of them. If we want all the details for a given pet, we must first find the **Pet Number** from **Pet** and then use that to look up **Breed** and **Vaccination** details from their respective indices.

Figure 58: Application side joins.

Denormalization

Denormalization refers to the addition of redundant data to a normalized data model which breaks the third normal form. In the case of Elasticsearch, it refers to flattening data during indexing, allowing each document to be independent. This is the intended use of Elasticsearch, which leads to optimal search performance. We remove the need for joins since redundant copies of the data exist in each document. The advantages of this method are fast query performance and works well with many-to-many relationships. The main disadvantages are that any updates in the data require costly reindexing, document size increases drastically requiring additional storage, and flattening data requires additional development effort. Figure 59 shows our Pet example through denormalization. The fields from breed and vaccination now are fields within arrays inside Pet. Note that the other two indices remain since joining happens during indexing and not querying.

Figure 59: Denormalization.

Parent-child

Parent-child document relationships are a good way to model one-to-many relationships. One of the key limitations is that both the parent and child documents share a single index and shard. As mentioned earlier, Elasticsearch API makes querying simple. The has_child function returns all the parent documents for a given child. Conversely, the has_parent function returns all the child documents for a given parent.

Some use cases where parent-child can be used are when the parent and child are separate documents, parent document updates don't require reindexing, child documents can be updated without affecting the parent document, and there is a significant volume difference from one entity to another in a one-to-many relationship. A few other limitations are that one index can only have one join field, one child can only have one parent since it is a one-to-many relationship, and queries can become costly due to the join. Figure 60 shows our Pet example in a parent-child construct. This is similar to our application side join, except all the documents are within a single index which could improve query performance. However, any update to the documents requires reindexing.

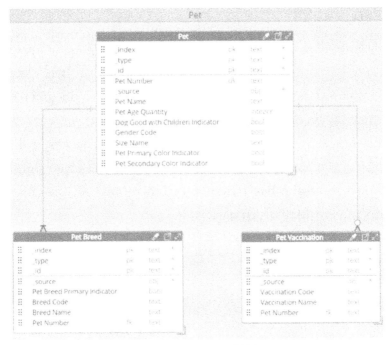

Figure 60: Parent-child.

Nested object

Nested object is a special type of object which allows arrays of objects to be indexed so that they can be independently queried. It is most useful when you want to maintain hierarchical relationships of objects in an array. The challenges are similar to the ones associated with denormalization: any update requires reindexing, and the object cannot be queried directly as it requires an explode function to break out sub-arrays and individual documents within them. Figure 61 shows our Pet example as a nested object. From an Elasticsearch perspective, all the data belongs to a single object, leading to a higher query performance than parent-child.

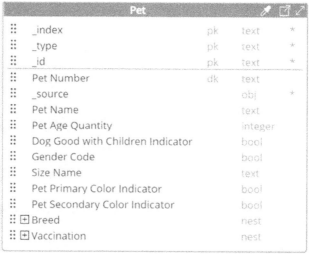

Figure 61: Nested object.

Table 8 summarizes the pros and cons of each modeling approach and gives some general guidelines on when to use which one.

Modeling Approach	Relationship Cardinality	Notes
Application side join	Many-to-many relationships	• Useful if you only have a few documents to look up. • Schema is easy to read and understand.
Denormalization	Many-to-many relationships	• You get to manage all the relations yourself. • Most flexible, most administrative overhead. • May be more or less performant, depending on your setup.

Modeling Approach	Relationship Cardinality	Notes
Parent-child	One-to-many relationships	• Children are stored separately from the parent, but routed to the same shard. So parent/children are slightly less performance on read/query than nested. • Parent/child mappings have a bit extra memory overhead, since ES maintains a "join" list in memory. • Updating a child doc does not affect the parent or any other children, which can potentially save a lot of indexing on large docs. • Sorting/scoring can be difficult with Parent/Child since the Has Child/Has Parent operations can be opaque at times.
Nested object	One-to-many relationships	• Nested docs are stored in the same Lucene block as each other, which helps read/query performance. Reading a nested doc is faster than the equivalent parent/child. • Updating a single field in a nested document (parent or nested children) forces ES to reindex the entire nested document. This can be very expensive for large nested docs. • "Cross referencing" nested documents is impossible. • Best suited for data that does not change frequently.

Table 8: Example of choosing between different document modeling approaches in Elasticsearch.

Creating an Index Mapping

As mentioned earlier, mapping is the process of defining the data type for fields in a collection that make up a document. A correct mapping is required to index fields and return search results as expected. Along with the data types, mapping allows you to set certain field characteristics such as searchable, returnable, sortable, how the data is stored, date format, whether the strings must be treated as full-text fields or not, etc. In Elasticsearch, you can define explicit mapping at an index level. If dynamic mapping is used (i.e., auto-detection), it can result in indexing failures, inaccurate data, or unexpected index search results.

Field Types

- **String**. You can save a string field as type, text, or keyword. The text type is used to index full-text values, such as the description of a product. These fields are analyzed by an analyzer to convert the string into a list of individual terms before being indexed. The text fields are best suited for unstructured but human-readable content. The keyword field type is used for structured content such as IDs, email addresses, hostnames, status codes, or zip codes, and the entire content of the field is indexed and searched as one unit.

- **Numeric**. You can use the numeric field types to define fields that hold numeric data. The various numeric field types supported include long, integer, short, byte, double, and float.

- **Date**. A field to hold a date type can be defined using the date type. This field can hold formatted date strings.

- **Boolean**. This field accepts the JSON values true and false. But, it can also accept strings that are interpreted as either true or false.

- **Object**. Use this field type for fields consisting of JSON objects, which can contain subfields.

- **Arrays**. This is a nested field type that can be used for arrays of objects to be indexed in a way that they can be queried independently of each other.

Characteristics

- **Searchable**. A searchable field is indexed, and the document containing the field can be searched and retrieved by the value of the field. The behavior of a searchable field varies based on whether the field is defined as analyzed or non-analyzed.

- **Returnable**. A returnable field is one which is stored, and the field value can be returned as part of the search response.

- **Sortable**. A sortable field is one, based on which the search results can be sorted in a particular order, either descending or ascending. The search results can be ordered by one or more sortable fields.

Schema validation

An important aspect, and often a limitation, of relational databases is that they operate on fixed, rigid schemas with a pre-determined structure of fields with known data types. Elasticsearch is much more flexible, as we've seen. But that does not mean that you should give up on data quality, consistency, or integrity.

Even in a flexible schema environment like Elasticsearch, where polymorphism is possible for different document types in a collection, validating documents being inserted or updated is a good practice. In essence, it allows you to achieve the best of both worlds: flexibility and quality.

Constraints may include whether a field is required or not, the data type or types for a given field, min and/or max values for numbers and whether negative values are allowed, min and/or max length for strings, value enumerations, the max number of array items, the structure of subdocuments, etc. You may even define polymorphic structures and whether unknown fields can be added.

Depending on the validation level specified, the database engine will strictly refuse to insert a non-compliant document or have a tolerant behavior of inserting the document while returning a warning message to the application via the driver.

JSON Schema is a powerful standard, but it can be a bit complex at times. Hackolade Studio makes it simple by dynamically generating the syntactically correct Elasticsearch mappings script without requiring any knowledge of Elasticsearch syntax.

This feature is not supposed to be a substitute for properly validating business rules in application code. But it provides additional safeguards to keep data meaningful beyond the shelf life of applications.

Monitoring schema evolution

Organizations operate in different ways. In many organizations following the principles in this book, data modeling happens in the initial stages of an Agile sprint or of an application change, then code changes occur and are implemented in the different environments. In other organizations, development has the upper hand, and evolutions tend to happen in a code-first manner. In such cases, data modeling can still come in handy to help with data quality and consistency. We talk about "retroactive data modeling" or "data modeling after-the-fact."

This process is useful to identify inconsistencies, such as the presence of addresses using the field "zipcode" while others use "postalcode." It is also critical to identify potentially more damaging situations in the area of PII, GDPR, confidentiality, etc.

Hackolade Studio provides a Command-Line Interface to programmatically invoke many of the features available in the graphical user interface. It is easy to orchestrate a succession of commands. In a code-first approach, the structure in the database instance evolves first. Every night, a scheduled process goes through the following steps:

- Reverse-engineer the database instance.

- Compare the resulting model with the baseline model. This produces a "delta model" and optionally a "merged model."

- A manual step allows us to review the model comparison and identify whether all changes in production are legitimate. Maybe adjustments are necessary to the code, or data needs migration.

- Commit the merged model, which becomes the new baseline model, resulting in publication to the corporate data dictionary so business users can be made aware of the evolution.

Schema migration

We have mentioned many times the great flexibility of the Elasticsearch document when it comes to easily modifying the schema as application requirements evolve. Compared to relational databases, achieving this with zero downtime, without the infamous migration weekends, or without blue/green deployments and other complex approaches is simple. We have also highlighted the need to leverage the schema versioning pattern to help applications process the data with the appropriate business rules and enable backward compatibility.

Challenges quickly arise in large and complex environments, particularly when multiple applications read the same data. It is not efficient or practical to port convoluted business logic to multiple applications for dozens of schema evolutions over time. It even ends up burning useless CPU cycles to handle them. And should we mention the risks of misinterpretation and misguided business decisions due to a query unaware of some specific schema evolution? New users of Elasticsearch discovering the flexibility of the document model often don't realize that it is a best practice in successful organizations to scrupulously perform schema migrations to reduce the technical debt of maintaining old schema versions.

There are several schema migration strategies to consider. The choice of strategy will depend on the specific needs of the database and the business, and careful planning and testing are essential to ensure a successful migration. Some organizations are even known to have developed costing models to evaluate the tradeoffs of the different strategies.

Schema migration strategies can be broadly categorized into two basic approaches: eager migration and lazy migration. There are also hybrid strategies that combine aspects of both eager and lazy migration.

- **Eager migration**: schema changes are made all at once, and the data is immediately migrated to the new schema. Similar to what has been done with relational databases, this approach requires more planning and may result in downtime during the migration process, but it ensures that all data is immediately updated to the new schema.

- **Lazy migration**: schema changes are made incrementally, and the data is migrated to the new schema only when it is accessed or updated. This approach can be less disruptive and easier to implement but adds latency to common operations. Furthermore, it is possible that all the data might never be fully migrated to the new schema.

- **Predictive migration**: schema changes are made based on predictions of how the data will be used in the future. This approach requires more planning and analysis but can minimize the latency in common operations.

- **Incremental migration**: schema changes are made in small, iterative steps, and the data is migrated to the new schema progressively.

Both predictive and incremental migration can be offloaded to processes running in the background or during off-peak hours to minimize systems impact. You may also combine strategies depending on the remaining data to be migrated: start with a predictive migration while doing lazy migration opportunistically, then finish with incremental migration.

Step 3: Optimize

Similar to indexing, denormalizing, partitioning, and adding views to a RDBMS physical model, we would add database-specific features to the query refinement model to produce the query design model. For Elasticsearch, data is indexed in every field with a dedicated and optimized structure by default. Most text fields are stored in inverted indices, while numeric and geospatial data is often stored in structures called BKD trees. There are also careful design and implementation considerations to be made to optimize Elasticsearch indexing performance. For example, don't index fields not used for search purposes. This will reduce the size of the inverted index and optimize the analysis of the field. Additionally, built-in field analyzers use significant resources and can slow down the performance of the index. It is good to carefully pick and choose the ones that are relevant. An example of a storage and retrieval barrier that can be minimized is using multiple threads. Using multiple threads to index will optimize data retrieval.

Indexing

Elasticsearch uses indices to improve query performance by reducing the number of documents that need to be scanned to satisfy a query. Some parameters to tune to optimize indexing include:

- **Tune refresh interval**: Set this according to your system requirements.

- **Disable replicas** if they are not required.

- **Automatic ID field**: Do not set the "_id" field of the document. If unnecessary, allow Elasticsearch to set the "_id" automatically.

- **Use multiple workers / threads to index.**

- **Use official clients**: Use official Elasticsearch clients since they have been designed to optimize the connection.

- **Avoid frequent updates**: Every update creates a new document in Elasticsearch and marks the old document as deleted. This can lead to several deleted documents and increase the overall size. To work around this, you may be able to collect all of these updates in the application used to call the index API to remove unnecessary updates and send only a few updates to Elasticsearch.

- **Index mapping**: Carefully design your index mapping. Don't index fields if they are not used for search (default is true), as this will reduce the inverted index size of Elasticsearch and save the analysis cost on the field. The index option controls it and can be modified.

- **Analyzers**: Use analyzers on your fields. However, note that some analyzers take significant resources and can slow down the indexing speed and significantly increase the index size of large text fields.

- **Wait_For_Param**: When there is a requirement to search the indexed document immediately, use wait_for_param while indexing instead of an explicit refresh.

- **Bulk API**: Use bulk API to index multiple documents instead of several individual ones. Bulk API performance depends on the size and not the number of documents in the request.

There are many reasons to use a data modeling tool to create and maintain indexing information, including better collaboration, documentation, ease of maintenance, and better governance. In addition to supporting all of the indexing options of Elasticsearch, Hackolade Studio also generates the index syntax so it can be applied to the database instance or given to an administrator to apply.

Sharding

We briefly discussed sharding. As a recap, data in Elasticsearch is organized into indices. Each index contains one or more shards. As data is written to a shard, it is periodically published into new segments on disk, making it available for querying. This process is called a refresh. Eventually, the number of segments grow and are consolidated into larger segments through a process known as merging. Shards are units that distribute data around the cluster. The speed at which Elasticsearch can move shards around when balancing and rebalancing the data depends on the size and number of shards and network and disk performance. Here are a few tips to optimize sharding and, in turn, query performance:

- Small shards result in small segments, which increase the overhead. Keep average shard size at least above a few GB. Common sizes range between 20 and 40 GB.

- Forcing smaller segments to merge into larger ones can reduce overhead and improve query performance. However, this is an expensive operation and should be performed or scheduled to be performed at off-peak hours.

- Use realistic data and queries to benchmark and determine the maximum shard size for query performance.

Generation of test data

Manually generating fake data for testing and demos takes time and slows down the testing process, particularly if large volumes are required. Using fake (a.k.a synthetic) data can be useful during system development, testing, and demos, mainly because it avoids using real identities, full names, real credit card numbers or Social Security Numbers, etc., while using "Lorem ipsum" strings and random numbers is not realistic enough to be meaningful. Alternatively, one could use cloned production data, except that it generally does not exist for new applications, plus you would still have to mask or substitute sensitive data to avoid disclosing any personally identifiable information. Synthetic data is also useful for exploring edge cases that lack real data or for identifying model bias.

With Hackolade Studio, you can generate first names and last names that look real but are not, and the same for company names, product names and descriptions, street addresses, phone numbers, credit card numbers, commit messages, IP addresses, UUIDs, image names, URLs, etc.

Data generated here may be fake but has the expected format and contains meaningful values. City and street names, for example, are randomly composed of elements that mimic real names. And you can set the desired locale so the data elements are localized for better contextual meaning. Generating mock test data is a 2-step process:

- One-time setup for each model: you must associate each attribute with a function to get a contextually realistic sample.

- Each time you need to generate test data, you define the parameters of the run.

Hackolade Studio generates the sample documents so they can be inserted in the database instance.

Three tips

1. Like many other NoSQL databases, Elasticsearch has a user understandability gap due to complex structures. It is highly beneficial as a communication tool to maintain the logical model

along with the physical, and make sure they are in sync.

2. Use metrics generated by APIs to get an idea of whether indices are stale. After some time has passed, some elements often make up an index that is no longer used or doesn't have data feeding into it. This will affect query performance and, in turn, requires reindexing.

3. Annotations or annotated text fields are a useful tool to bring in structured information into unstructured data for increased precision in text searches. Consider search-precision when choosing the appropriate physical data types.

Three takeaways

1. Indexing and query performance are the key drivers for the physical design.

2. There are four key methods of modeling data in indices for Elasticsearch. Pick the one that is fit-for-purpose and optimizes performance.

3. Keep Elasticsearch's built-in APIs and query functions in mind when designing the physical. These help optimize data storage and retrieval.

Index

www.ingramcontent.com/pod-product-compliance
Lightning Source LLC
Chambersburg PA
CBHW071245050326
40690CB00011B/2274